A. S. Hall

More About Communicating the Gospel and Halford E. Luccock

(continued from front flap)

a chapter on the Bible as a preaching sourcebook, replete with many hints for study and use. Technical aspects of sermon construction are taken up, keeping in mind the goal of transforming the person preached to. Finally, in the best "Luccockian" style, "Preaching During an Earthquake" discusses the real issues of our time and the preacher's clear function in relation to them.

With this book one of the great teachers of homiletics of this generation joins the select company of those whose wisdom on preaching is given permanent form in a famous lectureship, the Lyman Beecher Lectures on Preaching at Yale. The name of Halford E. Luccock may now be placed beside other members of the "royalty of the pulpit" as Edgar DeWitt Jones has called them: Lyman Abbott, Henry Ward Beecher, John A. Broadus, George A. Buttrick, Harry Emerson Fosdick, Charles E. Jefferson, John Henry Jowett, Charles Clayton Morrison, Reinhold Niebuhr, George Adam Smith, Henry van Dyke and many others.

For a quarter of a century Dr. Luccock was professor of homiletics at Yale Divinity School, retiring in 1953 as one of the loved and outstanding teachers of preachers of that period. Having met and witnessed in action most of the above-mentioned "royalty," he has imitated none and remains today one of the most inimitable and suggestive preachers in America. He is author of twenty books with this one, some of them classics in homiletic instruction, and writes a widely-quoted weekly column in *Christian Century*: Simeon Stylites.

Communicating
the Gospel

Communicating the Gospel

The Lyman Beecher Lectures on Preaching, 1953
Yale University

by

HALFORD E. LUCCOCK

Harper & Brothers, Publishers, New York

To the students of the Yale University Divinity School

1928–1953

whom it has been my privilege to teach

and with whom it has been my joy to work

Contents

Contents

Foreword

MOST of the material in this volume was given as the Lyman Beecher Lectures on Preaching at Yale University in April, 1953. To Dean Liston Pope and my colleagues on the faculty I am indebted for innumerable kindnesses, both during the lectures and throughout the years.

Parts of three chapters were delivered at the Pacific School of Religion on the E. T. Earle Foundation in February, 1953. My hearty thanks are given to President Stuart Anderson and to the faculty and students of the school for their generous interest and kindness.

I also wish to thank the following publishers who have granted permission to quote from copyrighted volumes of poetry:

Burns, Oates & Washbourne, Ltd. and Mr. Wilfred Meynell, executor, for the lines from "O World Invisible We See Thee" by Francis Thompson.

E. P. Dutton and Co. for the lines from *Gaily the Troubadour* by Arthur Guiterman.

Faber and Faber for the lines from *The Still Centre* by Stephen Spender.

Harcourt, Brace and Company for the lines from *Collected Poems* by T. S. Eliot.

Harper & Brothers for the lines from *Bolts of Melody,*

New Poems of Emily Dickinson edited by Mabel Loomis Todd and Millicent Todd Bingham, and from *Splendour in the Grass* by Audrey Wurdemann.

Henry Holt & Co., Inc. for the lines from *Last Poems* by A. E. Housman.

Alfred A. Knopf, Inc. for the lines from *Profiles from China* by Eunice Tietjens.

Little, Brown and Company for the lines from *The Complete Poems of Emily Dickinson*.

The Macmillan Company (New York) for the lines from *Collected Poems, 1951* by William Butler Yeats.

Macmillan and Co. (London) for the lines from *St. Paul* by F. W. H. Myers.

The New Yorker Magazine, Inc. for the lines from the July 8, 1939 issue.

Charles Scribner's Sons for the lines from *Tenor and Decorum, Poems, 1940–1948* by Peter Viereck.

The Viking Press for the lines from *Collected Poems* by Siegfried Sassoon.

New Haven, Connecticut   HALFORD E. LUCCOCK
July 1, 1953

Communicating
the Gospel

I

A Babel of Tongues

IT is a striking irony that our time, which has been called truly an age of communication, should have as a fitting symbol the Tower of Babel. The old Tower of Babel reached proudly into the air, but at its base was confusion of tongues. Our towers thrust up higher into the sky than Babel. But the radio and television masts on an Empire State building are baffling symbols of strange and obscure tongues.

Every day adds to the wonders of the means of sending messages. Man has outrun, or outflown, the sound of his own voice. The first issue of *The New York Times*, in 1851, achieved an amazing scoop. It printed news, rushed on the Royal Mail Steamer *Europa* to Boston, and by train to New York—news that was not much more than two weeks old. Today any morning we can read in the paper, not only what happened in Korea yesterday, but, by grace of the international date line, what happened tomorrow. Communication has created a new world, a new possibility of public opinion. Yet there is the deep mark of obscurity. Indeed, often listening to the world babel of tongues, we are tempted to think that the most powerful ruler of the world is Humpty Dumpty in *Alice in Wonderland*, who said in a regal manner, "a word means what I want it to mean." Russia is ruled by Humpty Dumpty, a mightier monarch than Ivan the Terrible. The words "peace" and "democracy" mean what the Kremlin wants them to mean, from day to day. The White Queen is powerful everywhere. We send out the Voice of America, but it does not come through to the mind of Asia, does not penetrate the thick wall of ideas and words. This pervades many realms of life.

All this is a twice-told tale. Its relation to our present theme is simple, to face the danger that the proclamation of the Christian religion may partake of the failure to communicate, the danger that what began as public speech may become the private language of a coterie. So it may fail to be good news to all men, and be merely one part of a Babel. There are so many varied forces in our day exerting pressures in that direction. We are concerned here with the extent to which that calamity to the gospel has happened and is happening. Milton's phrase, "dim religious life" may be applicable, not only to the interior of a sanctuary, but to the message itself—dim to the sight of multitudes.

This is urgent for three reasons at least.

1. *The very genius of Christianity is sharing, the conveying of a message.* The text for our whole theme might be the plea in the Epistle to the Hebrews—"To do good and communicate forget not." As the Revised Standard Version translates the word—"Share what you have." More than that, the gospel was not merely an idea, a message, but an idea in process of communication. We see it portrayed all through the New Testament in terms of motion. When it loses that motion of communication, it ceases to be itself. The disclosures of form criticism of the gospels

have enabled us to see the gospel, the message, formulated and shaped by the purpose of communication. Incidentally, form criticism does much for the morale of the preacher. It reveals that the preacher is not an excrescence, an appendage to the fellowship. He was not a Johnny-come-lately to the church. He was a prime mover. In the beginning was the word—the word of the teacher and preacher. Our gospels did not originate as histories or biographies, but as short theological sermons. So let the preacher drop his inferiority complex and lift up his head. He was there at the beginning of the drama, Act I, Scene I.

2. *Our time has put on the communication of the gospel a sense of urgency which is hard to exaggerate.* That urgency is portrayed in the title of a book which came from the Office of War Information shortly after the end of World War II. The title was *Persuade or Perish.* In some real ways that is the alternative before the church, persuade or perish. For the preacher that means that preaching is something momentous or it is an irrelevance. That same urgency for clear and lucid communication was vividly put in the first Christian century, "If the bugle gives an indistinct sound, who will get ready for battle?" We can say today, "If the bugle gives an indistinct sound, who will get ready for anything?" We have all heard pulpit trumpets which made reveille sound like retreat. The proclamation of the gospel is working against a deadline. Not that there is any final deadline to the action of God. But there is in the world's affairs a new apocalyptic age, in which the first-century exhortation has a new, intense meaning, "Brethren, the time is short." There is a disturbing timeliness in the words which the Fourth

Gospel reports Jesus as saying, "We must work the works of him who sent me, while it is day; night comes, when no one can work."* Night comes, or at least twilight, the twilight of the dark clouds of Bikini and Nevada. The time is short in which the response to the gospel can become a saving force against some impending threats. Behind all our preaching there is an audible obligato, the ticking of a time bomb.

3. The third compulsion to forceful clarity lies in *the power and effect of the enormous agencies of mass communication*. We have not yet begun to measure the present or future effect of the constant bombardment of the minds of today by all the agencies, radio, movies, television, the press, and print, all the way from the book clubs to the comics. They are speedily shaping a new portent, with which the conveying of the Good News must reckon, the mass mind. Not even Einstein mathematics could estimate the number of hours spent each week by a hundred million people, reading newsprint, listening to radio comment, watching television, or sitting through movies. A recent book on Africa bore the title *Ten Thousand Tom-Toms*. We have more than that in America, beating day and night. The process is something like an artillery barrage softening up an objective. Millions of minds are being "softened up," for what coming invasion we do not know.

Now, of course, we would be deaf, dumb and blind if we did not recognize gratefully the indispensable and great services which mass media render. The flow of news which

---

* Unless otherwise indicated, Biblical quotations are from *The Holy Bible, Revised Standard Version*, copyright, 1946, 1952, by Division of Christian Education of the National Council of the Churches of Christ in the U. S. A.

they achieve contributes to the functioning of society; the opportunities for recreation and entertainment make an immense contribution to living. Just to indulge in doleful denunciation of these major features of our day would be a futile effort to turn time backward, or in vivid picture, act like a disgruntled polar bear, sitting on a rapidly melting cake of ice, growling at the Gulf Stream.

Yet we would also be blind and deaf if we did not recognize the great new obstacles for conveying the Christian message which the prevalence of mass communication raises. It tends to shape a stereotyped, standardized mind. There is an inherent tendency toward uniformity. With the enlargement of communication there is very frequently the result, and always the danger, of mere diffusion rather than any distinction. The agencies of mass communication make easily possible putting over third- and fourth-rate stuff as authoritative and of high distinction. If *Forever Amber* is the choice of a book club it must, by that token, be great. If a hodgepodge like *Quo Vadis* cost seven million dollars to produce, and is a top box office bonanza, there is nothing more to be said. A shaping influence on millions of minds is that of movie directors aiming at the blood pressure of a twelve year old. All these instruments present a real threat to a capacity and habit which has been closely related to the promulgation of Christianity, the ability to read and the habit of reading. Will the ABC's give way to the wave length and the camera? In understandable exaggeration, Fred Allen has prophesied that the next generation will have eyes as big as cantaloupes and brains the size of a split pea; so much for the eye, so little for the mind. Much mass communication creates an atmosphere favor-

able to the acceptance of windy slogans as the ultimate
truth about life. Most dangerous of all, the situation where
one or a controllable number of views can be presented
simultaneously to large numbers of people lends itself to a
monopoly of ideas, or a single cultural pattern. It all greatly
sharpens the urgency for clear, competing communication
in religion.

Perhaps the worst thing about the mass media is the
banality of much that is presented. Like the brook, it "goes
on forever," day and night. Preaching must guard against a
carry-over from that. For the press, radio and television can
stand banality better than the speaker, for they have pictures, stage properties and music to anesthetize the pain.
But, if the blight of banality settles on the preacher, he
becomes a benevolent soother, "scattering sedatives and
sunshine, courage and quinine, aspiration and aspirin,"
bringing a weariness painful to be borne. To be sure, if
these lectures really faced the whole issue of mass communication, there would be much examination of the use of
these media in religion. There would be detailed explora-
tion of an immense opportunity. Obviously, I do not have
the knowledge or experience or skill for such a task. More-
over, it is not our present theme. It must be a major endeavor for the church today and tomorrow. All through
the Psalms there runs the plea to praise the Lord on all
kinds of instruments, the harp, the lyre, all that there were.
That plea must include the magical instruments of our day.
There is need for new musical instruments for the music
of the gospel. All honor to the pioneers who have gone
into this new territory, and all the help we can give to them.

One important aspect of this Babel-like lack of communication which makes at present a real hazard for preaching, is that in so many realms of life there is a lack of clarity and conveyed meaning. There is the danger we have already spoken of, that of creating a coterie, a supposed intellectual and artistic elite, a small segment of the possible audience, in which the mass of people hear very little either clearly or gladly. In many of the arts, poetry, music, painting and in scholarship, a private language has been employed, people writing and creating for one another, rather than using public speech. Obscurity has been elevated to the rank of a primary virtue.

There is very real danger that preaching, operating in the same world, subject to the same influences powerful in other arts and realms, may be exposed to the same blight. Much preaching has suffered the same opaqueness. It is a contagious disease. And note one difference between preaching and most other arts except teaching. The practitioner cannot make an easy retreat from failure to communicate into a snug fortress of disdain by saying, "These people are too dumb to get me." That rationalization has been used endlessly. It is always false and vicious. The preacher is commissioned to share a message and if he fails there, he fails, no matter what recondite and esoteric lore he may utter. May it be perfectly clear that we are not here attempting to evaluate what is called modern poetry, art or music. In all these realms I am the least of all the saints; far beyond that, we all recognize that there must be revolutionary change if an art is to live. An unchanging tradition petrifies. True salvation, abundant life, in any art is found in familiar words, "You have heard . . . but I say unto you." Death comes when men make void a living experience and expression, by a brittle tradition. We must remember that every new creation has been greeted with the words with which the poetry of Keats was greeted, in the massive judgment of the *Edinburgh Review*, "This will never do." Our concern here is with communication only, with the fact that right at the present hour so much in every art simply does not come through with recognizable meaning, and that preaching faces the same hazard.

In general, part of this cult of murky obscurity came from a revolt from the mass communication of the age. There is a disdain for what is simple and clear enough to be conveyed. Many writers, the incomprehensibles, are ashamed to be simple. They would lose caste. They disagree violently with Conrad who said that the purpose of writing is to make you see. The most complicated writing is often the most praised. The authors believe that "the true artist must hide from the crowd behind a thicket of briers." [1] Difficulty is demanded.

In poetry, difficulty has become for many the first ethical obligation. The obscurity is not that which legitimately inheres in great poetry from fullness of the subject and the poet's compression of language, but from a sort of house-party obscurity, an affair of private language and allusions meaningless and meant to be meaningless to outsiders. There is much merely cerebral jugglery. Some glowing words of the high priestess of the cult, Gertrude Stein, well described the effect, as far as communication is concerned: "Sound coming out of her had been sounding, and she had been telling that sound coming out of her—a sound that was sounding the meaning of something that was existing." There's no doubt about the sound! For a great host the reading of much modern poetry has ceased to be enjoyment and has become an exercise in crossword puzzles or the breaking down of a code. One of the plain people has thus voiced a natural complaint:

> What poets mean by what they mean
> Is harder than its ever been.
> Some say that Ezra Pound's the ticket,
> But I get lost in Ezra's thicket.
> I'm stumped by what the lilacs bring
> To T. S. Eliot in the spring.
> . . . .
> Alas, never will the masses know
> What Auden means who loves them so.[2]

Much modern poetry gets lost in its own psychic maze and the intricate game of words. As one of the advance guard, William Carlos Williams, has frankly put into a long poem the comment of one of his neighbors,

> Geze, Doc, I guess it's all right,
> But what on earth does it mean?

There is a shaky bridge between the poet and his audience. There is a classic story that used to be a joke. It is funny no longer. It is that of Douglas Jerrold, reading Browning's *Sordello*, and then crying out "My God, I am losing my mind!" It fits the present day too exactly. Against this, put the remembrance that great poetry has never been the private possession of an intellectual elite. Of course, we can say that this is only one form of art, and not in the field of religion. But who can say that some of the same tendencies are not operating in religion, in the overintellectualizing of a message, the incubus of a specialized language, the shakiness of the bridge between the pulpit and the public?

When we come to music, again we are not here judging modern music. Even the layman out on the farthest rim can be grateful for the abundant evidence that music is alive. Its vitality goes beyond mere repetition of the past. It is not on a merry-go-round. But at present so much of it does not come through with meaning to multitudes of music lovers. There is too much theory and not enough music, the same objection, by the way, that can fairly be made to some of our preaching, too much theory, not enough music. The danger of every revolution is that for a time, at least, it may issue in extravagance. That has happened in music. There has been technical extravagance. There is a lively little composition for the piano called "Kitten on the Keys." We have all listened to contemporary music which sounded more like "Hippopotamus on the Keys." We have been told by critics that we must acquire a toleration for what we now regard as ugly discords, and "forget all preconceptions of what melody ought to be."

What can we say of painting? What can I say that will not stamp me as a vulgar Philistine? Nothing, so I will go right ahead. Yet, I cling to the conviction that so much in the clashing modern schools of art, from abstractionism to surrealism, and even into darker shades of night, lacks any real element of recognizability. Hence it does not communicate. It is an artist himself, who says that "the minute the last ounce of recognizability has been squeezed from painting, it ceases to be art and becomes mere craft. The painter puts himself outside the realm of common experience. You might as well speak Coptic among the Lapps or Icelandic in Sumatra." If one who prefers Franz Hals's head of a "Fiddling Fisherman on the Beach" to Picasso's "Head of a Woman," which willfully destroys such forms as humanity has evolved in three thousand years of art endeavor, he is thereby a Philistine. Some modernistic art seems the product of throwing a huge gob of paint on the canvas, freely allowing it to drip down in rivulets as chance determines. One gifted painter of the surrealist school explains the process, "You simply go fishing in the subconscious stream: sometimes you catch a fine carp; sometimes all you bring up is an old shoe." There has been a brisk market for old shoes.

In scholarship, the partial failure of scholarship to meet the tremendous need for the communication of knowledge can be summed up in the words of an American philosopher that it is the business of a scholar to popularize knowledge. In that business there has been much failure. There has been too much limp and ready acceptance of the false division of writers and speakers into two kinds, the scientific people, who are the only ones who know anything, but cannot say it, and the literary people who can express themselves perfectly, but have nothing to say. That false division, accepted uncritically, has been disastrous in religion as in scholarship in other realms. There is a mean between dry rot and empty extravagance. One of the most hopeful things in the whole field of scholarship is that that middle way is being found. It is, of course, a vicious illusion that everything can be popularized, made simple and understandable to any casual bystander. More about that, accompanied by violent emotion, later. But on the other side, there has been a tendency of many scholars to build a spite fence around their subject, to make it more obscure than it is, impregnable to the battering rams of ordinary minds. So much scholarly work has been done in a sort of academic voodoo. So the question is asked wistfully, Has the race of scholars who can combine learning with narrative charm and a gift for the dramatic joined the dodo and the Brontosaurus?

Consider the field of history for instance. There has been a bitter struggle between the pedant and the artist in history, and for a long time in the nineteenth century, the pedant was winning. History had crawled into a hole. One man, scholar and artist both, George M. Trevelyan, thus describes it:

The reaction against literary history, as it was scornfully called, was rampant fifty years ago when I commenced historian. . . . History, it was agreed, was no longer to be written for the general reader and his likes: history books were henceforth to contain only the learned talk of historians with one another. If the public sometimes overheard that talk, so much the better, but that was a matter of secondary importance.[3]

Under the then dominant schools, history was driven out of the camp, like Hagar, into an arid wilderness of footnotes. But today the tide of battle is turning. We are witnessing a thrilling drama, the rescue by St. George on a charger, of the beautiful maiden, history, from the clutches of the dragon of sterile pedantry. There are many St. Georges making the rescue, men who are both scholars and literary artists, able to communicate learning with imagination, warmth and gift for drama such as Trevelyan, Churchill, Nevins and Commager, De Voto, Bainton and S. E. Morrison, to name but a few. But the battle must be carried on in religion as in other realms.

Part of the disastrous wall around learning has been

built of a specialized jargon. There is no need to whip that villain around the block again. He has already received his more than ninety lashes. But he is still alive, adding to the confusion of tongues, preventing the transmission of meaning. Here, we must be careful not to confuse necessary technical language in many fields with meaningless "Jabberwocky."

We may well heed the warning of Lewis Carroll,

> Beware the Jabberwock, my son,
> . . . .
> The Jabberwock, with eyes of flame,
> Came whiffling through the tulgey wood,
> And burbled as it came.

It does burble. So many writers and speakers, in their desire to become profound, succeed only in becoming polysyllabic. The words are not synonyms. There is so much that is buried in a tomb of official jargon—once called gobbledegook. But by any other name it reads as badly.

Take just a glance at the tragic lack of communication in the international realm, which is one of the greatest threats facing the world. Round-the-clock messages are sent out on the air. But so many are broadcasts from Babel. Much of the Voice of America has shouted to Europe and Asia the message that the United States is bathtub rich, that we have five times as many automobiles as the rest of the world, that our streets as full of traffic jams, that our people have the highest standard of living in the world. As one man in India has said, "Your broadcasts about the Good Life in America are like describing a State Banquet to a starving man." We have not communicated much persuasion. There are the continual obstacles to sharing ideas, the lack of a common language and understandable pictures. We have not established bridgeheads in Asia for a landing force of argument and persuasion. The result can all too often be described in the familiar words of Matthew Arnold on the East,

> The East bow'd low before the blast
> In patient deep disdain;
> She let the legions thunder past
> And plunged in thought again.

On the other hand, much of the Russian propaganda, full of lies and false cruel promises as it is, nevertheless is nearer to the grass roots, nearer to the experience of people and in the language they know. Looking at these other fields, the preacher may well say, with a sense of responsibility, "There, but for the grace of God, go I."

In this world, then, and in this atmosphere, subject to its various pressures, the preacher must operate. He faces the danger of taking on some of the obscurity dominant in many fields about him. He dare not be satisfied with the pleasant occupation of talking to a coterie in a rather specialized dialect. The preacher's craving must be that of Thackeray when one of his novels achieved a moderate success among the intellectually elite. It had what is called a success *d'estime*, a thin prize, too much like a moral victory in football. Thackeray was completely dissatisfied. He cried out, "My tunes must be heard in the street!" That must be the preacher's ambition. We must cry, "My tunes must be heard in the street!" Or rather, we must hear our Master cry, "My tunes must be heard in the street!" That is where they were heard in the first place. They were heard in the streets of little towns in Galilee, and along the roads. We read, "And the whole city was gathered about the door," and "There was no longer room for them, not even about the door." His tunes must be heard in our streets.

As a background from here on, may we remember this: Do not overestimate or underestimate the place and power of the sermon in the life and work of the Church. That power has been grossly overestimated. Much of Protestantism, historically, has laid on the sermon, as a chief or exclusive instrument of its work, a burden that it cannot possibly carry. Protestantism has made an unfortunate excursion into Greek mythology and came back with Atlas as the symbol of the preacher carrying the whole world of its work on the shoulders of his sermon. The load is too great. One of the blessed recoveries of our century has been to recognize the pulpit as one and only one, instrument among many. "The eye cannot say to the hand, I have no need of thee." The sermon cannot say to the fellowship of the Church, to worship, to nurture and education, "I have no need of thee." Maurice Egan has said that if the Protestant church ever dies, the dagger found in its heart will be the sermon. We can dismiss that as the judgment of a Roman Catholic, of sacramentarianism. But we ought not to shrug it off too lightly. For it does point to our grievous overestimate of the power of the sermon alone.

However, it is easy, and now in season, to underestimate the sermon as one instrument in the communication of the gospel. Jesus said there shall be no sign given but the sign of Jonah, the prophet interpreting the will of God. Dr. George A. Buttrick reminded us years ago that Jesus came

preaching. He could have done other things. He did other
things. He came preaching as a means of God's revelation.
As it was in the beginning it is now. There is a sound parallel to music. A critic [4] has recently written, "How tragically much the composer has to rely on the interpreter for
the realization of his purpose. For better or worse, music is
the produce of two agencies, and not of one, the composer
plus the interpreter." The preacher is the indispensable
interpreter of the music of the Song of Moses and the
Lamb. Resting on the unchanging experience of humanity,
the preacher need not fear even though he goes down into
the valley of the shadow of a mechanized age. In a time of
audio-visual aids, we may well remember that the greatest
audio-visual aid in all history was blind Homer delivering
poetry from the tail of a cart, a man speaking directly to
people. That is still the greatest show on earth.

The clarity of the preacher depends on many things. One,
certainly, is his knowledge of people, how their minds work,
how much and what they can effectually receive. It is not
the question which Ronald Knox condemns as being asked
by too many preachers, the question, "How much will Jones
swallow?" but rather, "How much can Jones understand?"
To ask that is our reasonable service, but all too often
omitted.

Here we must say again—we are not pleading for the
elimination of the mystery of the gospel. We are stewards
of the mysteries of God. The faithful steward will say with
Paul, "Behold I show you a mystery," and not denature it
into platitudes for retarded or tired minds. If anyone says
to you that you are preaching over his head, there is a good
answer in three words. Use it. It is, "Raise your head." The

trouble is most often not that preaching is over people's heads, but off to the side; not on the bull's eye of their interests or language. We read in the story of the Ascension that a cloud enveloped Jesus and took him out of the sight of the disciples. Without a knowledge of what people are prepared to receive, a cloud of words may envelop the truth and take it out of the sight of the congregation. Every Sunday may be Ascension Sunday on which the preacher takes off into the wild blue yonder of the remote and the abstract. The service may be like a day at the seashore. It begins in clear sunlight, the radiant objectivity of "Holy, Holy, Holy, Lord God Almighty," but by eleven-thirty when the preacher begins his sermon, a Newfoundland fog drifts in. Ceiling zero. Thomas Aquinas has a beautiful definition of God as "intelligible light." A sermon about God should have its full share of intelligible light.

May we all continually sit at the feet of one of the greatest teachers of preaching who ever lived. Strangely enough he never lived, except in imagination. He is, of course, Hamlet. I have often thought of having his address to the players printed in large letters and framed and put into the classroom.

> Speak the speech, I pray thee,
> . . . .
> Trippingly on the tongue;
> But if you mouth it,
> As some of our players do,
> I would as lief have the town crier
> Speak my lines.

The Master's lines have been all too often spoken by the town crier. How many ways there are of mouthing it!

Vocally, of course, spoken with the voice of a train caller, or worse, that of the perfect radio announcer, solemnly intoning the virtues of a breakfast food, with a frantic earnestness that ought to be reserved for Gabriel blowing the Last Trump. Mouthing it so that the wonders of God's grace lose all their amazement and turn into dull platitudes; mouthing it, till the word of judgment becomes a soft poultice of soothing words.

The classic word on this whole matter is that of St. Paul, "In church I would rather speak five words with my mind, in order to instruct others, than ten thousand words in a tongue." It is a nice little number, five. You will remember that David, in his battle with Goliath, chose as his weapons, five smooth stones out of a brook. And they landed, where ideas ought to land, in the head. Paul's five smooth words also land in the head. That word of Paul's spreads out over a preacher's whole life. For words can be in a relatively unknown tongue, both in ideas and language. There is a narrative in Mark which seems to me to speak emphatically to the preacher. Jesus healed a man who had an impediment in his speech. Then these words, "His ears were opened, his tongue was released, and he spoke plainly." That is the saving miracle in the pulpit; "He spoke plainly."

The lack of carry through may be in ideas, or language. My fear and conviction about much preaching of contemporary theology lies right here. Not about its validity, but that it is not communicated clearly, and so does carry sharp meaning to multitudes. One of the difficult things to persuade students in a theological seminary is that the classroom situation does not obtain in a congregation: that in a church they do not have a company of highly selected minds trained in theology and philosophy; or that the ideas and expressions which are a twice-told tale in the classroom are still Greek to the pew. Often the preacher's solo flights in the upper realms cannot be followed by the naked eye. So that often the preacher takes on the prerogative of the Pope. He excommunicates the whole congregation; that is, he puts them out of communication.

The preacher's mind may readily, like the dyer's hand, become subdued to the stuff he works in. Here, for instance, is a passage from a book by a brilliant and able theological mind:

Spirit is the union of being and nonbeing. Though reality is basically being, while there is nevertheless passage back and forth from being into nonbeing, as the perishing of cancelled time (from being to nonbeing) and the real creation out of nothing by the becoming of the genuinely new (from nonbeing to being) there must be a relation between the two realms of being and nonbeing which cannot be defined in terms of either realm without doing violence to its own kind of infinity. That relation, uniting within itself the two incommensurate and noncontradictory infinities . . . is spirit.

So help me, that is what the man said! Now you know what the spirit is.

Of course, two things are to be said. A nimbler mind than mine could readily grasp the truth. Also, the quotation is in a book of theological argument. However, that sort of thing carries over into sermons, particularly by the young. We have all heard it again and again. The safeguard is not to stop reading the work of real thinkers, God forbid. It is to use the same test that is regularly used by the director of a new play in rehearsal. He will stop the performance at a passage or line spoken and say, "That won't play!" His feeling is, it cannot leap the gap between the footlights and the audience. The preacher needs the same sensitivity, the quick ability to say to many an idea or passage, no matter how deep or beautiful, "That won't play."

Often ideas do not come through clearly because there is no subordination. They do not serve one master. The result is a tangle, with a result something like that of the woman who heard a series of lectures on Nazism, Freudianism and Confucianism, and came to the conclusion that Hitler's theory of the *libido* was due to the influence of Confucius. Or, nearer home, like the preacher who united Marx, Freud and Jesus in one all-comprehending muddle. Such milling around of ideas never brings people to the unifying experience of the mount of transfiguration, when they see no man, save Jesus only. They do not see, in shining light, the deed of God in Christ.

Two other things help to prevent the clear reception of ideas. One is the lack of definition. Definition involves the high art, worth a lifetime's dedication, of bringing an idea out of the everywhere into here. We have all heard people who interlard their conversation with a fuzzy "You know what I mean." I always feel like saying, "I don't know what you mean. Tell me." That is what a congregation, inaudibly and often unconsciously says, "Tell me what you mean."

May I suggest a project to those who are still students in this school? Someday when you have too much to do, that is, any day, go down to the Grove Street Cemetery and stand with head uncovered beside the grave of Noah Webster. And in that pious attitude think of the wonders of sharp definition, which Mr. Webster practiced so notably.

Definition is like making a clearing in a forest, enclosing it with a stout fence and saying, "This, exactly, is what I am talking about." It involves the ability, when you see an abstraction prowling around in the dark, to challenge it in the words of the soldier in Hamlet to the ghost, "Stand, and unfold yourself." For when vague generalities march back and forth in the pulpit, the minds in the congregation become a sort of no-man's land, that strange misty territory between sleep and semiconsciousness.

The other difficulty lies, often, in not knowing just how people take in ideas, what are the ways of the mind, how they best assimilate mental food.

A homely story which Ralph Waldo Emerson records has permanent wisdom. With the help of his son he was trying to get a calf to go into the barn. His son was pulling from the front and the great philosopher was pushing from the rear. Nothing happened, except that the calf was sing- ing, "I shall not be moved." An Irish servant girl, only a few weeks away from the old sod, came to the back porch and stood there laughing a moment. Then she went up to the calf, put her finger into its mouth, and gently drew it into the barn. She knew how her audience took in ideas. That calls not only for knowledge of people, but also for hu- mility, of sacrificing the joy of issuing papal bulls in our most infallible manner, and asking humbly, How may this truth reach these particular people? St. Paul was doing essentially that when he sought to be all things to all men.

A specialized language in the preacher is a high stout barrier to communication. It need not be highly technical or full of difficult words. It is enough to serve as a wall, if it is remote from the common speech of daily life. Recent

New Testament research has thrown much new light on the *Koine*, the common speech in which the New Testament was written. Its truth carries best in common speech. There is an illuminating passage in the 22nd chapter of Acts. Paul was in danger of his life from mob violence in Jerusalem. He starts his defense, and then we read, "And when they heard that he addressed them in the Hebrew language, they were the more quiet." When the message came in their own language and not in an unfamiliar tongue, they heard. It is always so. When language has no roots in human experience, when it offers no first aid to the senses, there is small response.

Tennyson's "Northern Farmer" was written almost a hundred years ago. But it is still tragically in date. The farmer is reporting his experience listening to the sermon, and his words, stripped of archaic dialect, still report an experience which happens in church all too often.

I 'eard 'im a-bummin' away like a buzzard-cock ower my head,
An' I niver knawed what he meaned, but I thowt 'e 'ad summat
    to say,
And I thowt 'e said what 'e owt to 'a said, an' I coom'd away.

"I coom'd away." That is the supreme anticlimax of the gospel. We can say that is only an imaginary ignorant farmer. Yet within a year I heard a man who is neither imaginary nor ignorant, one of the keenest lawyers in a great city, after hearing a sermon by a man under consideration for the pulpit of a church, say the same thing, in different words, "He seemed to approve of Christianity in spots, but we couldn't understand a blamed thing." What shall it profit a preacher if he gain a whole world of dialectic and lose his power to convey? It is not a question of the depth of thinking or ideas. A shallow brook six inches deep may be just as muddy as the Mississippi itself. Often it is a question of language, either stylized or just plain platitudinous. John Quincy Adams paid high tribute to the soporific language of Robert Treat Paine. He said, "He could make even murder tedious." It could be. I feel sure that most of us have heard preachers make even the greatest murder of history, the Crucifixion, tedious. In the pulpit the fear of the Lord is the beginning of wisdom, but the fear of unfamiliar jargon is a help.

Or, in regard to language, we may heed another word not in the dictionary, but it belongs in a preacher's lexicon, "Discocoon yourself."

To be fair, there must be one more entry in the ledger. The blame for low visibility of ideas and language is not all to be laid on the preacher, by any means. Many congregations must bear the blame, for they have put a high premium on windy oratory. In the pulpit there is often the rushing of a mighty wind. The Lord is not in the wind, but they love to hear it rustle. That is particularly true of that instrument of Providence, if it be such, the pulpit committee. Often it has a greater love of the ten thousand words in a tongue over the five clear words for the mind. For ways that are dark and for tricks that are vain, the pulpit committee is peculiar. So many times they listen for a certain set of hallowed noises. True, they follow St. Paul's injunction to try the prophets, but the scales on which they try them are badly out of kilter. I have known recently of a committee which heard two men on successive Sundays. The first was doing well a workmanlike job on a situation facing the congregation. The second was soaring into the upper air like Keats's Nightingale, higher still higher, giving forth profuse strains of unpremeditated words. The committee liked the sounds. They said, "That is our man. The Lord has spoken." They mistook the noise. It was not the voice of the Lord. It was merely a wind.

Many committees take very seriously the satirical words of *Patience:*

> If this young man expresses himself
> In terms too deep for me,
> Why, what a very singular deep young man
> This deep young man must be!

One great reliance, in the preacher's conveying his message, as well as the great compulsion is this: Looking unto Jesus the author and finisher of our speech, as well as of our faith. He was a sower who went forth to sow, concerned above all that the good seed of his word might bear fruit, in the soil of the mind. There is one passage where we can almost hear Jesus in the process of shaping a message. He seems to ask, "How can I make this clear?" He says, "To what shall I compare this generation? It is like children playing in the market places."

We would not be guilty of the wrong frequently done to Jesus, sometimes strangely enough, in perverted tribute, which reduces his thought and words to the naïve simplicities of a third-rate mind. No surer way has been found to distort Jesus than to fail to recognize his intellectual power and penetration. He dealt with traditional questions of religion and ethics with a profundity that was shocking to many of his contemporaries.

Nevertheless, Jesus spoke directly to the "great un-

washed." That is what they were, literally. They did not do
ceremonial washing. Jesus did not belong to the Judean
Institute of Arts and Letters. He wore no Old School Tie.
We can detect in the gospels some of the intellectual swank
and snobbishness which his preaching met. "The Jews mar-
veled at it, saying, 'How is it that this man has learning,
when he has never studied?' " [5] Jesus' first disciples met the
same sneers from the elite. The judgment of the elders and
scribes on Peter and John was that they were "uneducated
men." [6]

> It is the way the Master went.
> Shall not the servant tread it still?

This is a phrase, beloved of anthologists and publishers,
that describes the gospel—"in the public domain." That
means that you do not have to pay fees to the descendants
of Virgil and Shakespeare to quote their lines. They are "in
the public domain." So was the gospel. As it was in the
beginning, it must be always. One reason, among many,
why Jesus spoke as never man spoke, was his great concern
for the major issues of life as they pressed closely on people.
William Butler Yeats has pictured that gift in memorable
words, which might well be etched on the mind and
memory of the preacher:

> God guard me from the thoughts men think
> In the mind alone.
> He that sings a lasting song
> Thinks in a marrow bone. [7]

That may well be the preacher's prayer, to think in the
marrow bone of basic human experiences and hopes and
needs.

It is a fascinating journey to go through the gospels and find Jesus thinking in a marrow bone. The thoughts men think in the mind alone never disturbed him. When a scholastic issue was raised—the origin of evil, "Who sinned, this man or his parents, that he was born blind," from that arid speculation Jesus moves to the marrow bone of the man's predicament and need. His concern was not in the theoretical explanation of evil, but in transcending it. The thoughts men think in the mind alone, such as, "Is it lawful to heal on the Sabbath Day?" gave way to the marrow bone of life, "Take up thy bed and walk." We too may pray, "God guard us from the thoughts men think in the mind alone" and lead us into the marrow bone of the human plight.

In proclaiming this word, then, the preacher is a bridge builder. That is a notable title in religious history, *Pontifex Maximus*. The *Pontifex Maximus*, the great bridge builder, is the messenger who throws a bridge of clear communication across the chasm between the speaker and the hearer. We referred earlier to many modern poets building a shaky bridge between themselves and their possible audience. The gospel cannot go over a shaky bridge.

Of course, the communication of the gospel is God's activity. Never forget that. We must repeat here as we do in other realms of life and work—"I believe in the Holy Ghost." As St. Paul puts that basic truth for all time, "We have received . . . the Spirit which is from God, that we might understand the gifts bestowed on us by God. And we impart this in words not taught by human wisdom, but taught by the Spirit." If that truth drops out of the mind of the preacher, the pulpit is reduced to the ghastly predicament of living on its wits. And wits, no matter how sharp, are a vain thing for conveying God's saving word to the heart and mind. The preacher who depends upon his wits, either real or imaginary, on tricks or verbal novelties, or the child's play of exploding little homiletical firecrackers, has really filed a petition in bankruptcy as a herald of God.

But with that remembrance, we are to be channels of the Word. How shall a stream flow, without a channel? It is our reasonable service to clear the channel of obstructions which may block that stream. Or, to change the figure from water to bread, the miracle of preaching, in which, by God's grace, we have a part, is the miracle of the feeding of the five thousand. We did not create the inexhaustible bread of life. We are to break it into pieces and distribute it to people. I do not think there is any common figure with which the preacher may identify himself more usefully than that of one passing the bread of the communion table to a waiting congregation. That no doubt seems obvious. But what is not obvious is the fact, as I see it, that today it requires in the preacher an increasing amount of courage and devotion to accept the lowly role of the distributor of the Word. Other more seemingly exalted ambitions get in the way.

Dr. Samuel Johnson put with great wisdom the obstacle to communication which is created by a selfish concern for the elegance of one's style:

Every man speaks and writes with intent to be understood; it can seldom happen but he that understands himself might convey his notions to another, if, content to be understood he did not seek to be admired. But when once he begins to contrive how his sentiments may be received, not with the most ease to his reader, but with most advantage to himself, he then transfers his consideration from words to sounds, from sentences to periods, and as he grows more elegant, he becomes less intelligible.

One very great obstacle to communicating the gospel today is a curious perverse desire of many preachers to be known as profound. They use strange translation of the injunction of II Timothy 2:15, "Study to show thyself obscure." So many, in a frantic effort to be profound, succeed only in being muddy. This strange yearning to be difficult, and thus receive the accolade of incomprehensibility, has never perhaps been more frankly expressed than in the envious sigh of Hugh Walpole, the novelist, who wrote, "I'd rather be like Virginia Woolf than anything else on earth. How nice if people said, 'This new novel of Hugh Walpole's may be very beautiful, but we can't be sure because we can't understand a word of it.' . . . I'd truly love that." [8]

There are preachers as well as novelists who would truly love that! Yet no man can serve two masters. Let no pride of mind or of reputation seduce the preacher away from the task of being a messenger. Let the preacher be proud. Let him drop all benumbing sense of inferiority, but let his pride parallel that pictured in old words. "Let not the wise man glory in his wisdom, let not the mighty man glory in his might, let not the rich man glory in his riches." [9] Let not the wise preacher glory in his density or mystification, but in clarity to the wayfaring man. Let him lift his head in solemn pride, knowing that if anyone understands him, he is in a great succession; in fact, The Apostolic Succession.

Hear one conclusion of the whole matter. Communication depends on the force and the heat of the preacher's passion to evangelize. It all rests back on that. It depends on the depth of our conviction that the words we speak are matters of life and death, that it makes an overwhelming and eternal difference that our message be received. Without that headlong passion, all else is futile. It is something like the word which Barrie in *What Every Woman Knows* puts into the mouth of a Scotsman. When asked what "charm" in a woman is, he says, "It is something that if a woman has it, she doesn't need anything else, but if she hasn't got it, nothing else will do her any good." Now if a preacher has what used to be called "The passion for souls," he needs a great deal else. But if he hasn't got it, nothing else will do him any good.

I once began a course in preaching by reading the most exciting thing I know about evangelism, Browning's poem, "How They Brought the Good News from Ghent to Aix." I gave it all the dramatic effect I could manage,

> I galloped, Dirk galloped, we galloped all three.

In the language of understatement, the effect was less than perfect. But I still believe it belongs in evangelism. That poem gives a sharp feeling of two things which the carrier of the gospel needs, a compelling sense of urgency and a sense of people waiting eagerly through the night for good news. We can see the sparks struck out by the horses' hoofs; we can feel the speed.

> "Good speed!" cried the watch as the gate bolts undrew.
> "Speed!" echoed the wall to us galloping through.

The classic words are the familiar ones of F. W. H. Myers in his *St. Paul;* words that might well be pasted

among the pages of the preacher's New Testament. St. Paul
is looking at people.

> Only like souls I see the folk thereunder.
> Bound who should conquer, slaves who should be kings.
> Then with a rush the intolerable craving,
> Shivers throughout me like a trumpet call.
> O to save these, to perish for their saving,
> Die for their life, be offered for them all.[10]

Look at one word. I wish you could remember one word.
Shiver. Do we shiver, shaken with a trumpet call, that by
any means some lives may be made whole? Over the desks
of many of the broadcasters in London in World War II,
sending messages beamed to enemy countries, was printed
the question, "Is what you are saying worth a man's risking
his life to hear?" That is enough to rock any man back on
his heels. It is enough to rock the preacher back. Is what
you are saying truly a word of salvation, is it important
enough for a person to risk changing his life when he
listens? When we apply that stern test, how many of the
effects that we love so much, the silken words that we love
to stroke, are irrelevant! For a traveler along the road, it is
a far better thing to find a road sign, even in stark simplicity, than a painting by Picasso.

On a lower level, but still important for the preacher,
this sense of urgency will preserve the zest of preaching.
Without it the sermon so easily becomes just a weekly
chore to be dragged through. Then the preacher has
touched bottom, emotionally and spiritually. His Saturday
night dirge becomes "Tomorrow and tomorrow and tomorrow creeps on this petty pace" from Sunday to Sunday.
But if he is seized with the conviction that something

momentous is at stake, preaching can be an exciting wrestling match. It is a wrestling match, first, with an idea, if you can discover one, and second, with an audience, if you can get one. It is exciting, for both idea and audience can get away with all the agility of a greased pig. The thrilling question comes out, "Can I get a half nelson on this slippery audience?"

The glorious uncertainty of it keeps the mind on tiptoe. We can say with Ulysses,

> It may be that the gulfs will wash us down
> It may be we shall touch the happy isles.

The passion of an evangelist will save the sermon from that last indignity, that of having the deadly drip of a tired commercial.

This involves a tremendous thing, nothing less than actually believing that he that loseth his life shall find it. It is easy to say. It sounds rather well. But it is hard to believe to the extent that we build our work on it. For it involves subordinating every other ambition to what often seems the less glamorous one of making plain the way to God.

There is a word in the Epistle to the Hebrews which throws light on the preacher's renunciation. It is written in tribute to Jesus, "He made himself of no reputation." That is the last full measure of devotion for a preacher, to lose prior concern for his reputation; for in so many ways, his reputation is his chief, often his only, professional asset. It is his capital. He doesn't have much else. He doesn't have a home. He has lived his life in a parsonage. He doesn't have much in the bank, except a promissory note. All his eggs are in one basket, his reputation. It costs much to put aside the alluring reputation of an orator or a philosopher, for the calling of a herald. That means he resists the temptation to preach showily great sermons. Kipling has pictured the devil's supreme temptation in the field of art. When the caveman was daubing his first painting, the devil asked, "It's pretty, but is it art?" To the preacher, the devil's most seductive word is the word "great." The devil whispers between the pages of the sermon manuscript, "Oh, it may be useful, of course, but is it *great?*" To every preacher, the devil brings the third temptation of Jesus, with enticing contemporary trimmings. He says, "Do something dazzling. Forget about serving people. That's rather ordinary stuff. Fling yourself from the pinnacle of the Temple. Dazzle them. Get yourself a reputation. You can be immortal." In such a time, remember that noble figure of Greek mythology, Chiron, who was willing to give up his chance of immortality to save Prometheus. There is a New Testament echo of that. The preacher must be willing to forego his immortality, his reputation, if by any means he may save some.

Here is a bit of verse that says it all, and carries an authentic echo of the words of Jesus, "You know that those who are supposed to rule over the Gentiles lord it over them, and their great men exercise authority over them. But it shall not be so among you; but whoever would be great among you must be your servant." [11]

Here it is, "The Great Ones":

The Great ones brood aloft in calm benignity
    With book and pen;

We've thrust aside the scholar's dignity
  To live with men.

The Great Ones view the world with boundless charity
  From high above.
We work, we strive, we speak with vulgar clarity
  To those we love.

Before the Great One's shrines with due formality
  All Time shall bow.
We basely sacrifice our immortality
  To serve you now.[12]

II

The Faith Once Delivered—
Yesterday and Today

I DO not know who first invented the phrase, "the simple gospel." I hope that God, being slow to anger and plenteous in mercy, has forgiven him. But the evil that he did lives after him. For, hiding under the innocent phrase "the simple gospel" very often has been and is either a distorted or a denatured message. In discussing here the communication of the gospel, we do not mean that kind of simplification. Often that process has resulted in fantastic metaphysics or a set of easy moral maxims for tiny toddlers. St. Paul did not say, "Behold, I explain a mystery in words of one syllable." He said, "Behold, I show you a mystery." Often under the delusion of simplification, a church which is set to be a steward of the mysteries of God becomes a church of the Least Common Denominator. The gospel has often been simplified out of all recognition. It becomes, to use the alchemist's term, *caput mortuum*, deadhead, the residuum left after exhaustive distillation, when all that is valuable is taken away. We should remember in connection with the so-called "simple gospel" that when you take from anything that which makes it something, what you have left is nothing. It has been like the blighting "simplification" of other literature. In our own

46

day we have had a magnificent movie version of Kipling's *Kim*, in which nothing at all was missed except the whole point of the story. In like manner, the publishers of the book, *The Universe and Dr. Einstein*, received a request to be allowed to do a fifteen-minute simplified version for the radio. We have all heard similar thumbnail versions of the gospel.

Indeed, we are not far astray if we imagine the musings of Satan in the first century when he heard the apostolic preaching of Jesus and the resurrection. "That is bad!" he said to himself. "I cannot stop it. But I know a trick with two of that. I will simpify it." And he did. This does not contradict what has been said earlier about the need for clarity. An idea to be intelligible and relevant does not need to be simplified in the sense of amputating or distorting it.

This dilution and denaturing is partly an expression of the lure of the short cut, a predominant passion in America. We begin it in school with "pony" translations of Caesar, and go on to shorthand in ten days, dancing in six easy lessons, French in three weeks, "I can get it for you wholesale." So we have our short-cut, zip-along versions of the Christian religion.

Partly it is due to something deeper. It is a lack of faith in the gospel as a revelation of God, and a conception of it as something that has to be fitted into something else, if it is to have any authority. If it fits in snugly to the mood of the majority or the fashion of the hour, use it. If not, straighten out its unfortunate kinks and harmonize it. There is a stout legend that a young scientist called upon to perform some experiments before Queen Victoria thus explained the process, "The oxygen and hydrogen will now have the honor of combining before your majesty." They appreciated the honor and combined.

That is doubtless too good to be true. But it is not so very different from what has been said of the Christian gospel, over and over again in various periods. The stress and selection has clearly said, "The elements of revelation will now have the honor of combining to fit the ultimate majesty, the spirit of the time, the mood of the moment." Our message has combined in some very strange forms.

There is a characteristic instance of this, I think, in the phrasing of the topic of the forum on religion held at Smith College in February, 1953. The topic was "Faith on Trial. The Academic Mind a Challenge to Religion." We get a sort of picture of religion trembling at the knees before the academic mind. Of course, Christians are committed to give a reason for the faith that is in them, and to commend their gospel to every man. But that title gives a badly one-sided view of the situation. It is not only faith on trial, but the academic mind is on trial. Religion is a challenge to the academic mind. It was in the first century a challenge to the academic mind of Greece, which disdained the cross as "foolishness." It is a challenge today. Beethoven is not on trial before the high school glee club. Raphael is not on trial before the outdoor sketching class. Shakespeare is not on trial before the summer stock company. We can see from the vantage point of history that it was not so much Jesus on trial before Pilate, as Pilate and all that he stood for on trial before Jesus.

When we consider the word to be communicated, one thing becomes a duty preceding all others. That is to raise a *Te Deum* of Thanksgiving for the recoveries made by much contemporary theology. This is particularly incumbent on one who feels strongly, as I do, that some theological preaching today presents great obstacles to the effective communication of the gospel. But there can be no doubt of the measureless value to Christian preaching of the insights and recoveries of the chief theological movements of our generation. For which, now thank we all our God.

Karl Barth has put this in a way that is a first aid to the imagination in his words, "Whenever the church has told men of a tiresome little God, the churches are empty." This, of course, like so much of Christianity, is true only in the long run. In the short run we all know that some of the best-filled churches in America are those in which men are told every Sunday of a very tiresome little God, who is apparently chiefly interested in making people easy and comfortable, and where seldom is heard a discouraging word. But in a very real way, Barth is everlastingly right. There has been recovered for Christian thinking and living the God of the long run. A recovered text is "Our God is a great God." Not a tiresome little God, who is a useful appendage to the American way or any way or attached to any way, except His Own. A great God, not a mere purveyor of peace, poise and power to perturbed people.

These gains come from experience and thinking which are European continental in origin. It is easier to recognize them than to baptize them with a name. We learn on good authority that Barth is not a Barthian. Certainly the term "Neo-orthodox" has no sharp, definite meaning, not even as a missile in controversy. Coleridge's dictum applies to this name-giving procedure, "Make any truth too definite and you make it too small." It is hard to crowd into a name or description the gifts of the chief theological thinking of our time. Yet its nature is clear. It includes a newly realized Biblical theology, accepting historical criticism, but confronting the world with a new Biblical realism; and as a part of Biblical realism, superseding a romantic optimism about man by a more sober and realistic view of man as a sinner. This, with a renewed emphasis on the church.

The great recovery reaches primarily in two directions. A critic has said that the mind of Matthew Arnold missed two things, the glory and the horror of life. Those are two primary elements of the Christian faith, the glory of life, a transcendent God, and the horror of life, its sin, man's estrangement from and rebellion against God. When these go into low visibility, as they did over wide areas in prewar generations, the Christian gospel is not being communicated. No elaboration of skills can make up for that emptiness.

In regard to communication, a characteristic nightmare dream of the preacher has real significance. That is the dream of being in the pulpit without a sermon. Who of us has not had it and cannot remember its painful agony? It is really a sharper pain than the other common dream of falling from a roof. The reality to this dream is this, that without the dogma of the redeeming God we are in the pulpit without a sermon which has any adequacy for life. For what happens to the pulpit when that central dogma is dimmed? I think A. A. Milne has unintentionally given an accurate picture of the result, when he describes a child whose imagination lacks conviction. The child is not sure just who he is pretending to be, but still says "round about I go."

He was sure of only one thing—the round about. And the preacher who has no overwhelming conviction of the God who acts in Christ has as his only reliance the round about. So round about and round about and round about he goes, on the activities of the parish merry-go-round, motion without great meaning or goal.

This recovery of theology has, of course, been a gain from tragic experience. We have seen all too clearly what loss of faith in the absolute God has resulted in. Emily Dickinson put it concisely,

> The abdication of belief
> Makes the behavior small—
> Better an *ignis fatuus*
> Than no illume at all.

That is a history of fifty years in four lines. There was an abdication of belief, resulting in very small behavior. It was an insane world, in the Egyptian use of that word. For the Egyptian considered insanity a flight from God, in which the ego, fleeing its destiny, journeyed into the void and built a world of its own. That is what happened to the world, 1914 and 1939 and the interlude between, a flight from God and a journey into the void.

A classic expression of the relation of faith in the Christian God to life is found in the prophecy made about one hundred years ago by Heinrich Heine. Writing of Europe and particularly of Germany, he said, "Once the taming talisman, the Cross, is broken, the savagery of the old battlers will flare up again, the insane berserk rage of which Nordic bards have so much to say and sing. The talisman is brittle. The day will come when it will pitiably collapse. The old stone gods will rise from the forgotten rubble, and rub the dust of a thousand years from their eyes, and Thor will leap up and his giant hammer start smashing the Gothic cathedrals." [2] What Heine called the talisman of the Cross did fail, and Thor did smash the cathedrals.

A memorable footnote to this whole matter is found in the way in which so many prophets of hope have become the prophets of doom. One little microcosm in which we can see what happens in a much larger world is the mind of H. G. Wells. His slide from the summit of optimism to the deep pit of abject despair is a demonstration of an inevitable process, that when a man begins by believing he can do everything by himself, he ends up by believing he can do nothing. Wells was the last great exponent of the nineteenth century's optimistic rationalism, with its faith in the perfectibility of human life, through science and enlightenment. In that faith he was the exhorter and cheer leader of a generation. He demonstrated how a secular utopia easily turns into a secular eschatology with a frightening vision of last things. Wells rejoiced that man had become a new animal who can jump a thousand miles, see through a stone wall, bombard the atom and analyze the stars, yet he complains that man goes on behaving like the weak, quarrelsome little ape he used to be. Wells's only remedy is to say, "Stop being an ape." A good idea but something is lacking! In his last years Wells went into a despair more bitter and savage than anything in Dean Swift. In his last book, *Mind at the End of Its Tether*, he puts the whole universe into the bankruptcy court. He wrote, "The human story has already come to an end . . .

and *homo sapiens* in his present form is played out. The stars in their courses have turned against him, and he has to give place to some other animal better adapted to face the fate that closes in more swiftly upon mankind. . . . Our universe is not merely bankrupt; there remains no dividend at all; it is not simply liquidated; it is going clean out of existence." [3]

So ends, inevitably, a godless utopia. One popular text of recent years has certainly been retired. It was "Beloved, now are we the sons of Darwin and it doth not yet appear what we shall be." The trouble is that in two wars it began to appear exactly what we should be—cinders on a cinder heap. Christian thinking has helped us recover the only alternative to that, an old one, "Beloved, now are we the sons of God." The half gods go, God arrives. In his light we see light. We see in his light that the substitutes for the absolute God are futile and shabby idols. We see that the new Messiah, so ecstatically hailed by the Pentagon and other headquarters, "Buck Rogers," and his shattering machines, bring no salvation. Even a more respectable substitute, democracy, is a vain thing for safety.

We can find the true symbol of the futility of liberal democracy without Christian affirmations of faith around the green of many a New England city. The buildings represent a Holy Trinity—the bank, the insurance company and the industry. From that comes the creed, "I believe in compound interest and keeping up dividends." [4]

One tremendous recovery needs only a word of statement—the recovery of a sharp sense of sin, of the dark power of evil. Much of this recovery can be put in the old, old sentence, "The world's train of progress is not late;

there has been a wreck." That is what Biblical realism is all about. It begins with a recognition of a malady—"We were dead through our trespasses." Face that tragic fact as the New Testament faces it. The beginning of a cure must be the recognition of the real disease. That is true all the way from a tuberculosis sanatorium to a meeting of Alcoholics Anonymous. One hopeful mark of our time is that the depth of that malady is seen not only by the theologian but by many poets and other writers. St. Paul started the custom of recognizing good theology in the poets. We can safely follow him. Here is Siegfried Sassoon:

> Chained to the wheel of progress uncontrolled;
> World masters with a foolish frightened face;
> Loud speakers, leaderless and sceptic souled;
> Aeroplane angels, crashed from glory and grace;
> Deliver us from ourselves.[5]

It is an insight that goes back to Wordsworth, but too often forgotten during the ensuing century. And how terribly these words fit our world today:

> But at the surface of things, we look, we hear
> Of towns in flames, fields ravaged, young and old
> Driven out in troops to want and nakedness
> Then grasp our sword and rush upon a cure
> That flatters us, because it asks not thought
> The deeper malady is better hid;
> The world is *poisoned at the heart*.

There is an immensely interesting parallel between theological thinking and much literary interpretation of the world today. Both have escaped the bog of romantic sentimentalism in a realistic appraisal of evil in man and society. There is a profound sense of the abyss under the surface

of life in fiction and poetry as in theology. It is found in the
violence, the cruelty, the horror, of O'Neil, Jeffers, Faulkner, Koestler, Kafka. It is no accident that our time has re-
discovered and reappraised Herman Melville and the tragic
sense of life that he profoundly felt.

In view of the need for communicating this revelation,
we do well to be painfully weary of having the gospel presented as a useful help in supporting anything else, *anything*. I have elsewhere given permission to anyone to
shriek aloud whenever Christianity is trotted out as an instrument in defeating communism or preserving democracy
or doing anything except confronting man with God. Just
as many of us got very tired years ago of religion being
hailed as a help in winning a war. God was reduced to being
an Assistant Secretary of War, or a minor subdivision in
the Department of Civilian Defense.

Here, for instance, is the president of a great university
(not Yale; I am broadminded; there are other great univer-
sities), a few years ago, opening a conference on Christianity by saying that it is good to present the objectives of
Christianity in an age when, and I quote, "the humanistic
values of Western civilization are being threatened by ma-
terialistic philosophy." It is all true, but must we always
bootleg the Christian revelation into the world, introducing
it surreptitiously as a useful backing for "the humanistic
values of Western civilization?" The whole subject really
belongs more fittingly under the title of an old book,
Civilization—Its Cause and Cure. For some of the so-called
"values" of our civilization are just what is the matter with
us.

Now we come to the other side of the picture and ledger.

On it I speak briefly but from strong conviction. Yet with real fear and trembling, for the sea of theology is great and my boat is small. Valid criticism must be brought to much preaching of contemporary theology, or the so-called Neo-orthodoxy, for its overcompensations for previous-existing deficiencies.

Overcompensation is one of the commonest features of the processes and progress of thought. A vivid picturing of that is found in a persistent legend from Dublin. The father of Oscar Wilde was a distinguished eye specialist, Sir William Wilde. The father of Bernard Shaw went to him to be treated for a cast in the right eye. That was corrected and cured. It was so completely cured that for the rest of his life, Mr. Shaw had a cast in the left eye! It all goes back to Luther, who has given a pungent picture, as he has of so many things. He said that humanity was like a drunken peasant. Prop him up on a horse, and he falls off on one side. Prop him up again and he falls off the other.

I am not now evaluating the theological validity of many of the theological emphases, which, as they come through in much preaching, are one-sided stresses. In the field of theology, my amateur standing has never been questioned. I do not hold a card in any theologian's local, either A. F. of L. or C. I. O. Also remember that our concern here is from the standpoint of effective communication. Also, I am considering here now, not the original thinkers, not the sources of ideas and movements, so much as the preaching that stems from the sources, most often that of the neophytes, and acolytes, who are always more extreme than the major prophets themselves. From the standpoint of sharing and conveying meaning, and of persuading, the opaque, murky character of much preaching does not come alone from obscurity of language and form, but from the message itself.

First, the doctrine inherent in much current preaching is stronger on sin than it is on redemption. Far more stress has been given to diagnosis than to therapy. Often it stops short of the end of the General Confession. There is rightful stress on "we have erred and strayed." But there is far fainter emphasis on "that we may hereafter live a godly, sober and righteous life." In the seventeenth century there was a much more exact knowledge of poisons than of remedial forces. So in much preaching of the continental emphases in theology, there has been better knowledge of destructive than remedial forces. This has been noted and pointed out by Professor Daniel Williams in his *God's Grace and Man's Hope.* There has been more specific and vivid treatment of Romans 7:19, "the evil that I would not, that I do" than of II Corinthians 5:17, "If any one is in Christ, he is a new creation." If what we have is a continual reiteration of man's "innate sinfulness" without an adequate stress on the saving grace of God and the sustaining power of the Spirit, we do not communicate the whole gospel.

Again, much preaching of current emphases in theology *is fractional in its disparagement or disdain of reason.* It has overcompensated for an arid rationalism, by what has at times amounted to a contempt of reason. The precious recovered truth is, of course, this, as expressed by Coleridge, "The highest truths are those which lie beyond reason." We find it in Charles Wesley's hymn,

> The things unknown to feeble sense
> Unseen by reason's glimmering ray,

With strong commanding evidence
Their heavenly origin display.

True, but to what does the "strong commanding evidence" appeal, if not to reason? John Locke's warning has a timeless pertinence, "He who destroys reason to make room for revelation, destroys both." "Faith and reason are companions of an infinite journey." Jesus did not disdain reason. Again and again he brings his truth to its bar. "How does it seem to you?" "Which of you that is a father?" "If you then, who are evil, know how to give good gifts to your children, how much more will your Father who is in heaven give good things to those who ask him?" In other words, it stands to reason. Without leaving a real place for reason in religion, we cannot fulfill the commandment to "love God with the mind." We are not to leave our minds outside of the sanctuary, as the Mohammedan leaves his shoes outside of the mosque. There has been great loss to the persuasiveness of the Christian message among large hosts of people, when the old discipline which used to be called Apologetics went into low visibility or was discarded, for much Neo-orthodox preaching seems to take for granted the very things which multitudes of people regard as being up for discussion. This is particularly true in the colleges where the big question is not only, "What is the Christian message?" but even more emphatically, "Why should an intelligent man believe it, or pay any attention to it?" Among too many preachers it has not been fashionable to answer that question. If we are truly to communicate it had better become fashionable again. For the earnest plea in the First Epistle of Peter is never out of date—"Always be prepared to make a defense to any one who calls you to account for the hope that is in you."

Once more, the strong *affirmation of the transcendence of God* in Barth and many others has been a needed message. That insistence is that the word of God comes into human life from a realm which is sundered from human life, yet brought near to it by Christ Jesus. That was much needed when the transcendent sovereignty of God was almost lost in a mist of humanism. What has been called the "new naturalism," for instance, denied nearly all disjunction between God and nature and conceived of God as one aspect of the natural world. There had been too *little* discontinuity between God and nature. But in the correction of that there is often too *much* discontinuity. The gap between God and his creation is made too great for man's need, and for the Biblical conception of God, the Creator. While affirming transcendence and passing over immanence, many have passed lightly over the Fatherhood of God and the love of God. A God who is "wholly other" easily becomes a deistic God. Such a conception loses some of the fundamental features of God revealed in the prophecies and Psalms and especially in the gospels, the God who clothes the grass in the fields, who numbers the hairs of our heads, and is so revealed in Christ that he that hath seen the Son hath seen the Father. While God is sovereign, it is the sovereignty of Fatherhood and of love.

Again, the recovered sense of sin comes through in much preaching as a devaluation of man. Salvation begins by the operation of grace, but it is wholly unwarranted to distort that truth to deny any good in natural man, or to say, as some have said, that all social effort for betterment is futile till God intervenes. That is a denial of the operation of the Spirit of God in human life. It is a falsely pessimistic view of human nature. It is ironical that thus Christian theology is made to join in the devaluation of man which is a mark of so much thinking and acting today. It colors so much current literature which swings from hopelessness to cynicism, and a loss of faith in human nature.

William Watson is near the truth when he writes that we come "magnificent out of the dust . . . and abject from the spheres." "Magnificent" and "abject"—both words root deeply in the Bible. We need not be ashamed to look at man through Browning's eyes:

> Oh, we're sunk enough here, God knows,
> But not quite so sunk that moments
> Sure, though seldom, are denied us,
> When the spirit's true endowments
> Stand out plainly from its false ones
> ....
> There are flashes struck from midnights
> There are fire-flames noon days kindle.[6]

There are in man heights as well as depths, tenderness as well as degradation, sacrifice as well as brutality.

The 8th Psalm proclaims of man, in the Revised Standard Version, "Thou hast made him a little less than—" what? The word *Elohim*—"a little less than *God*." A. A. Milne puts into the mouth of a child the words,

> If I were God, I'd be very proud of man.

There are many times when that is blind romanticism. There are many times when that carries an echo of the New Testament. "Of whom the world is not worthy." "Therefore, God is not ashamed to be called their God" (A. V.). (Note, almost Milne's exact words). "They shall walk with me in white, for they are worthy."

Look at another opaque window, which prevents the full light of the gospel coming through, in the note of hopelessness about the world and the future, unintentional in purpose, which sounds from some preaching. The needed preaching of dependence on God may be so extreme that it overlooks the other end of the bridge between God and man, man's responsiveness. We do well to realize that a horse is a vain thing for safety. All of man's glittering achievements are a vain thing for safety, without God. "Except the Lord build the house, they labour in vain that build it" (A. V.). But, that has too often shaded over into a paralyzing "What's the use?" Edward Shillito's parody of many years ago, a parody of William Merrill's hymn, "Rise Up, O Men of God," was very unfair to a whole theological movement, but it does echo much preaching which has exaggerated that insistence on dependence. It was, you remember,

> Sit down, O men of God,
> There's nothing you can do.

Often the Christian message, instead of being a counterforce against the despairing pessimism, so widely experienced in life and expressed in literature, becomes a parallel to it. Even at times, it seems to be a part of it. There is no need to labor the mood of hopelessness in literature. Samuel Hoffenstein's parody of the pessimism of A. E. Housman strikes a familiar note. Of his three friends in Gotham, one was dead, one had palsy, and one would soon end up in Sing Sing.

To that, the antiphonal response is not "Let us pray" but "Let us throw in the sponge." Preaching has become with some a sort of a Wailing Wall, with no hope till the final catastrophe. We must not forget that just as distorted a vision may be glimpsed through the green glasses of pessimism as through the rightly despised rose-colored glasses of optimism. With both, we see through a glass darkly. Our gospel must be preached in such a way that men feel "our labor is not vain in the Lord." We are called to labor in hope. May we preach in that remembrance, so that it will not be incongruous to sing after the sermon,

> Lead on, O King Eternal
> The day of march has come.

Or even,

> Rise up, O men of God.
> The Church for you doth wait.

For without the sense of hope in the human effort, in the struggle, we leave out a whole New Testament dimension of our faith, "We are laborers together in God." "Fight the good fight." It is a dimension pictured memorably in Bunyan's Mr. Valiant,

I fought till my sword did cleave to my hand; and when they were joined together, as if a sword grew out of my arm. And when the blood ran through my fingers, then I fought with the most courage.[7]

As another obstacle to the imparting of the Christian message, many certainly would include in some contemporary preaching a *distinct minimizing of the priority of Jesus in that message.* Here again, part of the reason, at least, was a needed correction of the extravagant claims and expectations of the "Jesus of History" school a generation and more ago. That school felt that scientific historical criticism could yield the full portrait of the mind and personality of Jesus Christ. There was reiterated a distorted distinction between the Jesus of History and the Christ of faith. One sad effect of this was the emergence of a "Jesus Cult" or "Christism," a sentimentalizing of Jesus, not as a revelation or incarnation of God, but as a substitute for him.

But, correcting that, there has appeared in some theologians a distinct lack of interest in the historical Jesus. They are not strongly interested in the Jesus who teaches in the Synoptic Gospels but only in the dogmas about him. Barth, for instance, attaches the unusual adjective "commonplace" to Jesus. He writes, "Jesus Christ, in fact, is also the Rabbi of Nazareth, historically so difficult to get information about, and when it is obtained, one who is so apt to impress us as a little commonplace, alongside more than one other founder of a religion, or even alongside many later representatives of his own religion." [8] Jesus—commonplace alongside of Mohammed, or Augustine! That is extreme, of course, but the position has found its way into preaching. As one scholar, Professor Samuel Terrien, has given a forthright picture of the trend in his words:

A number of Biblical teachers and preachers, especially in Europe, but also in the English-speaking world, have stepped on the neo-orthodox bandwagon with such alacrity, that they tend to disregard the historical character of Biblical revelation, as if they had been able to delete the phrase, "under Pontius Pilate" from the Symbol of the Apostles. [9]

G. K. Chesterton has written that there are many people today who know the last word about everything and the first word about nothing. The last word in Christian theology may be this, that or the other person. The first word is Jesus.

After that detour we are back on the main line, which is a *Te Deum* of Thanksgiving for a new grasp on an overwhelming gospel. For that is the purpose of revelation, to overwhelm the mind of man and his will to rebellion and to overcome the world. From here on we consider some compulsions which must be laid on the heralds of that message if it is to be communicated in any overwhelming way.

That calls for theological preaching with a dimension of depth. For modern society is what Professor Tillich calls it, an eccentric world, a society which has lost its spiritual center. And when man loses God as his center, he loses himself. From another viewpoint the terror of our time has been that primitive man has returned. He must be met with primitive Christianity. This calls for more than the preaching of doctrine. That could be done by indoctrination, a not too difficult task. Of course we need the preaching of doctrine. But merely to announce the doctrine in solemn tones is not to convey it. That is a trouble with some preaching by theological students and young graduates. They are entranced by points of doctrine, and they mistake the announcement of these points with confronting the congregation with the good news. What is merely stated is never presented. We must convey the reality to which the doctrine points—God. And who is sufficient for that? In that task, we cannot be reminded too often that it is the duty of a shepherd to feed the sheep and not to entertain the goats.

A commonly used phrase may lead us, I think, in this communication of God. It is the phrase "He rang the bell." Used, as it often is, of a preacher, it usually has a vulgar meaning, indicating that he did something sensational, had a personal triumph of some sort, flung himself from a pinnacle and dazzled the audience. But there is another, and a high, meaning of the phrase. It comes from the Roman Catholic celebration of the Mass. It is a high moment for the believer, who accepts the Roman doctrine of the Mass, when at the elevation of the host a little bell rings, signifying the presence of God. That is our calling, brethren, to ring the bell in that high meaning, to communicate the sense that "this is none other but the house of God, and this is the gate of heaven" (A. V.).

We cannot communicate the gospel if we fail to express the astounding wonder which is at the heart of the revelation. That, all too often, is the lost dimension of preaching. It represents an unchanging need of the human mind and heart. Ours is today a world surfeited with facts and information and entertainment but deficient in wonder. We have an unending parade of novelties, but with a "rapidity of things going stale." It sounds like a paradox, and it is, that a world full of wonders has lost the sense of wonder. The two are quite different. We gape at a bewildering succession of marvelous machines but there is little of the deep amazement felt on the Judean hills so long ago.

> When I look at thy heavens, the work of thy fingers,
>   The moon and the stars which thou hast established;

> What is man that thou art mindful of him . . . ?
>
> . . . .
>
> O Lord, our Lord,
>   How majestic is thy name in all the earth! [10]

One reason why religion, to many, becomes flat, stale and wearisome is that the sheer wonder is left out.

> The things that cannot be, but are.

We may hear the drumtap of rationalism and common sense, but no horns of elf land faintly blowing. Life is truly measured, not by the number of breaths taken, but by the breaths not taken, when breath is stopped, by the moments of breath-taking astonishment and amazement. This is the breath-taking wonder of our faith, that God himself has stepped into our life, with its suffering, calamity, fear and sin, and the inevitable dissolution of death, and has redeemed it. If we do not convey what is found all through the New Testament, the sense of astonishment, we are reduced to careful moralizing which is often ethically mean. A poet has given the verdict on that.

> I fear this careful art will never storm the sense.

There is a disturbing suggestiveness in the common phrase which we use all the time, "A nine-day wonder." It seems to warn cynically that there are so many things to which the limit of wonder is nine days. Then the astonishment changes to the commonplace and familiar. That may be true of life itself, with its trailing clouds of glory.

> And by the vision splendid
> Is on his way attended.
> At length the man perceives it fade away
> And fade into the light of common day.

Marriage can be only a nine-day wonder, dwindling down into merely a tired friendship, and often the tiredness is more evident than the friendship. So the shades of the prison house of routine may darken even the light of the glory of God in the face of Jesus Christ till that is only a nine-day wonder. There is no warning to any of us more imperative than this, "Watch out for the tenth day!" For the tenth day comes. Watch out for the busy day when wonder fades.

> New every morning is the love
> Our waking and uprising prove.

New every day is the unspeakable gift. And new every day must be the rebirth of wonder. John Jay Chapman says that the first thing to do with Shakespeare is not to pocket him, or to analyze or dissect him, but to say, "Oh, oh, oh!" like a child looking at fireworks. Pray that you do not lose your exclamation point. It is a means of grace. There are plenty of "Oh, oh, oh's" in the New Testament. St. Paul kept watching fireworks—"O the depth of the riches and wisdom and knowledge of God! . . . To him be glory forever!"

Preaching, like all true religion, begins in the passive voice, not the active. "Not that we first loved him," but that we are loved. If we are not first convicted, we do not convict anyone. If we are not forgiven, we do not forgive. If we are not ourselves amazed, we do not amaze anyone. Give yourself a few moments of excitement sometime, following that word "amazed" through the New Testament. The concordance can be a terribly exciting book. It all began that way. "And amazement seized them all, and they glorified God and were filled with awe." [11] And on through Acts, "They were filled with wonder and amazement." [12]

Christianity made its way through the Roman world by the communication of wonder. A man fails as a preacher if he is not an Ancient Mariner, home from the sea, holding an audience by a magical tale of astonishment.

> O wedding quest, this soul hath been
> Alone on a wide, wide sea.

There must be the experience of startled awe, felt all through the New Testament, "Behold the Lamb of God"; "See what love the Father hath given us that we should be called children of God; and so we are."

John Donne saw it clearly and puts it in one word.

> Take me to you, imprison me, for I,
> Except you enthrall me, never shall be free.[13]

"Enthrall" is not a common word. Many people are interested in Jesus. They are stimulated by him, inspired by him. They are not enthralled. Yet, it is the only adequate word. This wonder of the gospel cannot be communicated or shared without strong emotion. Not without far more emotional drive than is frequently brought to it. That word "emotion" is suspect, and rightly; a much more accurate word no doubt is "intensity." If wonder is the lost dimension of preaching, intensity of feeling and proclamation is often a lost power. We need waste no time stressing the obvious truth that raw emotion has been and can be the greatest power for evil in the world. We have seen what happens when peoples begin "thinking with the blood," which Hitler loved so well. Milton has the perfect phrase, used in another connection, "comes the *blind fury*." That is what it has been, "a blind fury." A rush of emotion can be a paralysis of the brain and a coronary occlusion of the heart. Yet, our emotional nature is a gift of God; and we dare not forget that when emotions are enlisted under the right banner—which is a primary task of Christian nurture—they are a measureless power.

Hasn't there been in preaching too much confinement to the middle register of the emotions, all in good taste and highly refined? I am not pleading for a revival of the "campmeeting jerks." Although I do know some churches—and they are not all in New England either—which could do very well with a few cases of "the jerks." There is a realm of power which is often missed, between two frightening extremes, that of emotional starvation, where the sermon is a sort of Phi Beta Kappa address, and on the other end, an emotional riot. Two processes of history in the last two generations should be etched into the memory of the Church. There was a time when it was quite a fashion to give up specific creeds and formulations. Then along came Marx, the creedalist, with an economic Nicene Creed, with a power which we haven't yet begun to measure. A cloud bank of foggy phrases is no match for that sharpness of creed, however false we know it to be.

So, also, just at the time when churches were throwing emotion out of the window as not intellectually respectable, along came Freud, picked it up and recognized it as the driving force of life. With too many of us the classic definition of poetry goes into reverse. It is not "emotion remembered in tranquillity," but emotion *forgotten* in the tranquillity of good taste. Shall we earn that highest tribute which the eighteenth century could pay to a preacher, that he was "pious, without enthusiasm"? Our sermons in the temple may move decorously from point to point, but there is not enough "walking and leaping and praising God." Perhaps the miracle—a cure for spiritual arthritis, is not complete.

A policeman friend of mine stopped me in the midst of a street traffic one day and asked, "What is the degree which many preachers have which makes them Doctors?" I said, "It is usually a D. D." His face lit up. He said, "That's funny. That is the commonest entry on every police station blotter in the country, 'D. D.' It means 'Drunk and Disorderly.'" I got safely out of traffic before reeling from that blow. Then my thoughts went back to the book of Acts. It is remarkable that those were the two charges continuously brought against the first heralds of the gospel. They were charged with being drunk. At the very beginning the charge was entered, "They are filled with new wine." [14] And they were called "disorderly." "They dragged some of the brethren before the city authorities crying, 'These men who have turned the world upside down have come here also.'" [15] In the beautiful Christmas play, *A Child Is Born*, by Stephen Vincent Benét, a serving maid at the Bethlehem inn says, "The shepherds were drunk with the good news." I wish I could say to all of you, in solemn tones, "By virtue of the authority committed to me, I confer upon you the Degree of D. D.—drunk and disorderly." That, in figurative terms, is a very honorary degree. Without it we are not in the Apostolic succession. Here preaching must obey two of the basic laws of propaganda. First, reiteration, line upon line, over and over, and second, passionate affirmation.

Emily Dickinson has a thrilling description of a remembered sermon—it

> Deals one imperial thunderbolt
> That scalps your naked soul.[16]

Now let's be realistic. We do not expect much scalping to be done at the eleven o'clock Sunday morning service. Though, even there, could there not be a few more scalps taken? Could there not be more blood raised to the scalp, so that the mind and heart might tingle with strong feeling? But it is not as common as it may have been a hundred years ago. Yet we can pray, "O God, may we keep some of Thy thunder." There were "sons of thunder" among the disciples. They belong there. There is a wonderful petition in the prayer hymn,

> Take not thy thunder from us,
> But take away our pride.

There is true insight there. For it is often pride, intellectual pride, cultural pride, which robs us of something really out of this world—God's thunder.

Again, it is obvious—but like so much of the obvious, it is easily forgotten—if we are truly to communicate, if there is any real sharing of religious experience, we must have religious experience to share. That truth is vividly expressed, in the words of Peter to the lame man at the temple gate—words spoken at the very moment of the communication power—"Such as I have I give unto thee" (a. v.). Nothing else. There is nothing on earth harder than to give to others something we do not have. We are called to be witnesses to the gospel. But if it has not really *happened* to us, we have nothing to witness to. That is true in a law court. We have all seen the lawyer watching a witness for the other side of the case, crouching like a tiger in the underbrush, waiting for such words from the stand as "I think," "I have heard," "I suppose." Then he leaps on the victim with three savage growls, "irrelevant, incompetent, immaterial." It is. And such witnessing is as incompetent and irrelevant in the pulpit. We can truly witness only to what has happened to us. Willa Cather made a true observation on literature when she wrote that the peculiar quality of a first-rate writer can never be defined but only experienced. That truth reaches out from literature into the Christian religion. Christ can never be completely defined. The Son of man hath not where to lay his head in any neatly defined scheme of thought. He can only be experienced.

We cannot escape the truth that no doctrine can live in the intellect which does not renew itself in experience. Where the witness of the Church has been faint or futile, that truth explains the failure. For instance, all too often the doctrine of the one family of the one God has not been renewed in experience, and as a consequence, it has not lived in the intellect, and the witness of the Church in race relations has been faint. The philosopher Croce has said truly of the writing of history, "The deed of which the history is told, must vibrate in the soul of the historian." If we are to tell the story of the deed of God in Christ, that deed must vibrate in our souls. Without constant vibration of that experience all the possible arts and techniques of communication are trivial and futile. Lacking that vibration, we become like those versifiers who have been called the "week-end school of poets," people who live in an apartment in New York, and dash out to Westchester or Connecticut on Sunday, see a daisy, and hurry back to the city to write a sonnet about it. Unless one lives with nature, the verse can be pretty thin stuff. And the week-end school of preaching, a Sunday dash into the pulpit, for a half an hour of eloquent hearsay, can be just as thin. Here is the source of prophetic communication, "I saw the Lord, . . . high and lifted up." [17] "I know whom I have believed." [18] "If any one hears my voice and opens the door, I will come in to him and eat with him, and he with me." [19]

Two things follow from this. One is the overtone of preaching, the most hopeful thing in Christian communication, the conveying of what is not specifically said. That, by the grace of God, happens. If we do not believe it, we had better not preach at all. For then we would have to depend on our wits, a frail reed to lean on. In that truth of the overtone, we are in the realm of the action of the Holy Spirit, which takes the things of Christ and brings them to men's remembrance, far beyond any specific things the preacher has said. It is the miracle that through a man's poor, lisping, stammering tongue, truth and experience which are not exactly named can be conveyed and felt. It is like an overtone in music, the double octave. That is what it is, the overtone of the music of the song of Moses and the lamb. I think that is part, at least, of what happened during the first Christian sermon at Pentecost. We read that people of many tongues heard in their own language. They felt the reality of God's disclosure, through the action of the Holy Spirit. In that high sense, Pentecost is a reproducible experience.

The second thing is like unto the first and underlies all true preaching. Communication is a two-way process. If there is to be a communication of God's message, there must be communication *with* God. Freely ye have received, freely give. It is all in the military axiom, "The secret of victory is in keeping lines of communication open." Does an invisible Companion go with us, so that that perfectly staggering promise of Jesus is fulfilled, "He who receives you, receives me"?

That calls for the discipline of prayer that we may be transformed by the renewal of our minds. Some years ago, in looking over a list of strange-sounding names of Puritans, I saw one name I envied. It was not anything so fantastic as Strong-in-the-Faith-Brown. It was simpler and better. One man was named Renewed Robinson. It sounds alluring, doesn't it? "Renewed." We may all be Renewed Robinson, if we pay the price. That high pattern of life is found in the parable of Jesus, which seems to me to be peculiarly the preacher's parable—the friend at midnight. A man was asked suddenly to provide food for others and realized that he himself had none. So he went to one who had much to give and said, "Friend, lend me three loaves; for a friend of mine has arrived on a journey, and I have nothing to set before him." [20] Every day the preacher has friends who have come to him from a journey. Often a hard journey over rough roads. Of ourselves we have nothing to set before them to sustain life. Those words must live on our lips and in our minds and hearts, "Friend, lend me three loaves."

III

To Serve the Present Age

MAY we begin with William James. He wrote, "As long as there are postmen, life will have zest." We need not delay long to document that proposition. You know the emotional difference between first- and second-class mail. You know the letdown which comes when you are expecting to get a letter from home and receive a circular advertising a soap or a dictionary or shirt instead. William James was not writing about preaching. But his word goes to the center of it—the task of giving to theological affirmation the zest and directness of a personal letter.

We should never forget the earliest Christian documents were letters; the message was first conveyed in letters addressed to people. It should never lose that personal letter quality. For when it does lose it, it loses zest terribly. Unless there is some kind of a personal address to the message, it is undelivered mail.

There is unfairness in the common jibe—all jibes are unfair by their very nature—that the churches are very good at answering questions that nobody is asking, but are not answering the questions that everybody is asking. But there is enough truth in it to make us watch and pray. Some are in the position of the theological student, who, as an assignment in systematic theology, did a very effective paper on

"A Dialogue with a Pantheist." Two years later he complained that he did not find any pantheists in the Bronx.

An English artist was sketching outdoors in the Barbizon District in France. He was at work at his easel set up along a stream, when a group of four children appeared in front of him and watched every stroke of his pencil. Finally one said, "Mister, please get us in the picture!" That is exactly the plea, earnest, though unspoken, which the congregation says to the preacher, "Get us into it." Right there we can be deeply grateful for the service which the present strong interest in personal and pastoral counseling renders to preaching. It has helped the preacher enormously to get people into the center of the picture in his preaching. Without that, there is no preaching, no matter what floods of words are turned loose.

So, when we consider sharing and conveying a message, one first axiom is that preaching is not spraying the universe with words, but bringing a message to people. Emerson's words on this matter are old and well worn. But so, for that matter, are the Ten Commandments. We cannot recall them too often, for they go to the mark like a well-aimed arrow. The golden word for preachers: "Cease, O thou unauthorized talker, to prate of consolation and resignation and spiritual joys in neat and balanced sentences, for I know these men who sit below. Hush quickly, for care and calamity are things to them. Here is Mr. T., the shoemaker, whose daughter has gone mad, and he is looking up through his spectacles, to hear what you may offer in his case. Here is my friend whose scholars are leaving him and he knows not what to turn his mind to next. Here is the stage driver who has jaundice and cannot get well. Here is Mr. B., who failed last week, and he is looking up. O speak things to them, or hold thy peace!"

But when, by the grace of God, we do speak things, the sound, in a poet's phrase "is like that of the axe when it goes into living wood."

We must heed the injunction given to opera singers to face the audience and not sing into the wings. When we do face the audience in our thought, we see the needs that are there. Here follow swiftly just a few of them. Needs that must be before our eyes, if we are to serve the present age. We take our stand by the roadside where Jesus stood when the human parade went by, trying to see it with his eyes, "When he saw the crowds, he had compassion for them, because they were harassed and helpless, like sheep without a shepherd." [1] Go down any street. Knock on any door and we will see some of these needs. The gospel has a saving word for each of them. But for the present just look at them.

1. _There is an oppressive sense of insignificance_ felt by many. Currency has been inflated but one's sense of personal importance has been deflated. Amid much inflation, modern man has been losing his individuality. On an assembly line he too closely resembles a cog or a number. In many other roles there is a feeling of separateness and not counting. It is not only in the army and navy that men are expendible. In much thinking and writing the Economic Man has been superseded by the Statistical Man. And the role of a statistic is not a happy one. A traveler reported a few months ago an incident in a railway station in Glasgow which throws a beam of light a long distance. A train carrying many factory workers was about to leave in the morning,

when a shrill cry from a woman calling to her husband was heard. "Wait!" she shouted. "We have forgotten our *non-entity* cards!" Of course, it was easy to see what she meant was "identity cards" which workers in the factories were required to carry. But it is a notable phrase, "non-entity cards." We all carry a non-entity card, do we not? In these days of great impersonal forces running over the earth like gigantic tanks, we have pressed on us the feeling of being "non-entities." What does one person count? An astronomer looks through the 200-inch telescope and says, "That shows how small and insignificant man is." There is your non-entity card!

2. There is the sense of insecurity, of anxiety, of fear. We know all too well and shudder at what is called "parasitic insecurity," the desire for a leader, which has turned loose rivers of blood in the world. It is a sort of projection of a childish "mother knows best"—the leader knows best. Anxiety and fear are reflected in so much of our current American literature. They spread out from economic insecurity to the whole circle of life. Worries and fears roll steadily off the assembly line of the mind. We can understand it and sympathize with it. For we feel much of it ourselves.

3. Then there is the sense of emptiness, to be seen and felt in so many. Old values are gone and there are no replacements. Eugene O'Neill calls it the major theme of our time, the "death of the old God and the inability to find anything to take its place." The traditional world has collapsed and a satisfactory new one cannot be created. The mark of a large part of this generation is not rebellion so much as a painful lament for lost certainties and a fumbling

search, through a blindfold, for a new faith. Contemporary literature has made many moving presentations of this emptiness at the center of life. Here is T. S. Eliot in *The Waste Land*:

> What shall I do now? What shall I do?
> . . . What shall I do tomorrow?
> What shall I ever do? The hot water at ten.
> And if it rains, a closed car at four.
> And we shall play a game of chess,
> Pressing lidless eyes, and waiting for a knock at the door.[12]

We find the same question in F. Scott Fitzgerald: "What will we do with ourselves this afternoon?" said Daisy. "And the day after that, and the next thirty years?"

4. There is the feeling of the futility of life and the absence of hope. Sometimes that is largely a popular pose, wallowing in a muck of defeatism. But in many people it is real. The feeling expressed in Hardy's *Tess* is present in many. Poor Tess is looking at the stars. Her companion explains that the stars are like apples, some good, some blighted. She asks what kind of a star the earth is. "We live on a blighted one," was the answer. Psychiatrists have discussed this host of people who are on the borderline of happiness, men and women for whom life has lost its savor, but who plod along, often hugging their discontent to themselves, who cannot realize their own lives, but add much to the uncertainty and unhappiness of others. These are the people for whom Edna St. Vincent Millay speaks in the line, "Life must go on. I forget just why." They find a voice also in A. E. Housman:

> Yonder see the morning blink
> The sun is up, and up must I

To wash and dress and eat and drink
And look at things and talk and think
And God knows why.[3]

With some that reaches the extreme of a bitter despair.
Hobbes has come back to Earth with his picture of life as
"solitary, poor, nasty, brutish and short." Today's literature
has drawn searing pictures of the futility of life, empty of
character and purpose. Even Noel Coward is a stern moral-
ist in that sense. But many authors, like him, have no meta-
physic, so there is nothing to do but make a protest. One
could go on, as we all must, exploring the geography of
need and sin.

There is much in this map of need that spells Christian
opportunity. For many needs are distinctly felt. When that
happens, it presents the best teaching opportunity. The
time when people really learn is when they really need
something. There is a great host of people who are not
saying, "I will arise and go to my Father." But they have
gotten as far as the barnyard, and they do not like it and do
not want to stay and dine on husks. They feel and say,
"There is something wrong about life. It does not taste
good. It does not add up to what it might." There we can
learn from Philip the Evangelist, and his meeting the
Ethiopian treasurer. Beginning at a specific point of need,
we read, "He told him the good news of Jesus."

One inescapable compulsion is laid upon us, to see and
hear. If we are to bring help to need, we must know the
tensions which people are under. Our minds must be sensitive plates on which are recorded the tensions of a generation.

In this connection, Professor Tillich has rendered great

Christian Obligation

service to all the churches in his effective insistence that
there is no real communication of the gospel without par-
ticipation in the experiences of our generation. We must
make our own, the prayer,

> May my tone
> Be fresh with dewey pain alway.

Stephen Spender has expressed his powerfully:

> Oh let the violent time
> Cut eyes into my limbs
> As the sky is pierced with stars that look upon
> The map of pain
> For only when the terrible river
> Of grief and indignation
> Has poured through all my brain
> Can I make from lamentation
> A world of happiness
> And another constellation.[4]

The "terrible river of grief" must pour through us. That will
save us from the unforgivable sin of remoteness. In a crowd
going down any street one must be able to see not only a
mass, but the different walking experiences. It calls for
dedicated eyes and imagination. There are three cars going
along, the wedding car, the funeral and the "Black Maria"
of the police department. There is a boy anxiously going to
his draft board, and a girl going to a physician to learn the
results of a tuberculosis test. There is one couple trying to
borrow money for a down payment on a house, and another
buying a casket. "Each face, dear Lord, a world."

We need a spiritual radar, or, to change the figure, the
skill to read the invisible ink in the lives of people. Sharing
is a two-way process. We must hear as well as speak, if the

speaking is to have any saving word. We may not have what the psychoanalyst calls the third ear, but two ears will help, if they are open. There is a grace of listening which is also a power. We hear often the familiar words concluding a radio program, "Thank you for listening." There is deep meaning to the words for us all. To give one's whole and serious attention to another person is a great gift. Recall how Jesus always stood at attention before a person asking for help, often when all his disciples could think of was "Send them away." I think much of the appeal of palmistry lies right here. While people are getting their fortune told, they are at least getting the complete, concentrated attention of another person, which, unfortunately, is a rather rare thing. So, the preacher's head cannot say to his foot, "I have no need of thee." He cannot say, "Let the lower orders do the footwork." The feet that take him into paths that people travel become organs of speech. Remember, it was "the feet of him that bringeth good tidings of peace" that were blessed.

Preaching, as we have said, has found a new and powerful ally and instrument in the interest in pastoral and personal counseling. It has done much and will do more in helping the preacher come to a sharper focus in his sermons. A real interest in counseling and skill in it will do much to save preaching from the ever-present danger of mere verbalizing. It will save us from deserving the tribute paid to the speeches of President Harding, "an army of pompous phrases, moving over the landscape in search of an idea." Words are the preacher's glory. They may also be his ruin. Counseling helps the pulpit move more directly into the teaching methods of Jesus. He did most of his teaching to small groups or to one person. He spoke to their condition. Whether he was rebuking Simon the Leper at the dinner table, or saying to the rich young ruler, "Go, sell all you have," it was a counseling ministry aimed at a person with a particular need.

The practice of counseling makes it possible to go on preaching year after year in the same place without tiresome repetition. Life itself presents an inexhaustible variety of experience, and the preacher who ministers to life finds freshness. It is the congregation itself which is the renewing force in the mind and work of the minister.

There is one caution. We earnestly hope that the well-justified exhortation against direct counseling, as opposed to the greater effectiveness of nondirective counseling, will not be taken as all the Law and the Prophets on the subject. That can be followed too slavishly. Some preachers have become so reluctant to appear dogmatic, so hesitating to give direct advice, that they end up by giving little or no help at all. The message becomes a sort of Delphic oracle, a holy noise issuing from a cave and hard to interpret. So they lose the affirmative quality of the gospel. If the taboo on all direct counseling had been in effect when the first Christian sermon was preached at Pentecost, when the people, deeply moved by Peter's words, asked, "Brethren, what shall we do?" he would have had to say, "Well, you'll have to figure that out for yourself." Peter did not know any better than to give some direct counseling, "Repent and be baptized in the name of Jesus Christ." At the conclusion of the parable of the good Samaritan, Jesus said, "Go and do thou likewise." That was suspiciously like direct counseling. So when the disciples made a direct request of Jesus, "Lord, teach us to pray," he made a direct answer, "When you pray, say, 'Our Father. . . .' "

Bringing the resources of Christian faith to individual need—that is, pinpoint preaching rather than saturation bombing—calls for one immense caution. Take the aid which psychology gives without allowing it to become a dilution of, or substitue for, the gospel. That is a very real danger. We live in psychological days, in which the ears are bombarded with psychological terms. One woman, sitting under the ministry of an up-to-date preacher, got the impression that the libido was the devil. Perhaps she was not so far wrong in that! Another person thought that psychosis and neurosis were two women in the Bible to whom St. Paul sent his greetings, like Tryphena and Tryphosa.

The popular psychologist, which frequently means the charlatan, has become the medicine man and soothsayer to millions. He has, of course, invaded literature. Thus David Seabury takes apart Hamlet: "He had a broken mother tie, a suppressed father fixation, erotic ambivalence, hidden gynephobia and a huge frustration complex." [5] Exit Shakespeare. The vogue has reached over into religion. A great many within the churches, and in the pulpit, while piously repeating theological phrases, take their sanctions from psychological prescriptions.

There is no need to reiterate at this late day the immeasurable service which a valid psychology has rendered to religion. It has enabled man to take the greatest step forward in fulfilling the injunction "Know thyself" since that command was given back in Greece. It has furnished priceless help in making religion effective by revealing the forces and mechanisms which move the mind and spirit and turn the wheels of life. Psychology can help to interpret religious experience and channel it. It cannot create it or be a substitute for it.

But with some preaching of today, the psychological emphasis has been the camel in the tent, crowding into a corner or clear out the rightful occupant. A continuous stream of sermons on how to be healthy, wealthy and wise has kept people holding their own pulse and taking their temperature. The attention is too much centered on the audience, on themselves, while the high and holy object of religion—God—goes into a cloud. This modern Pilgrim's Progress is not a journey to the celestial City of God, beginning with a load of sin falling from the back, and continuing in a life-and-death struggle with sin, but a pleasant little ramble to self-expression and success. There has been much one-sided veneration of adjustment as a *summum bonum* in itself, as though the chief end of man were not to glorify God and enjoy *Him*, but to get rid of all tensions and enjoy *yourself*. Of course, there is a grace of adjustment to life's conditions which is a central in Christian experience. St. Paul realized it, "For I have learned . . . the secret of facing plenty and hunger." [6] But the passive kind of adjustment, urged by many, seeks, however unconsciously, to take the saving tension out of life. It is like looking at the works of a watch and saying, "Poor little main spring, all bound up and tense. Loose it and let it go." But when you take the tension away from a watch, it is no longer a watch but a useless assemblage of junk. Take the tension out of life, the dissatisfaction, the striving, and you have the same reminder, an assemblage of junk. Some preachers have discovered a new verb which seems to have superseded the old ones. "Strive to enter in at the strait gate" (A. V.). "Follow." "Sacrifice." It is the lovely verb "relax." They preach from a very *much* Revised Version of the New Testament. "If any man will come after me, let him take it easy," or, "Go ye into all the world and keep smiling."

The Christian faith is degraded into being just an instrument—a sort of glorified aspirin tablet or a headache powder. Such a synthetic "gospel" recalls the words of Peer Gynt, "Well, that's what I call Christianity! Nothing in it to make one feel uneasy. Indeed the theme of the priest's address—that we should all strive to be ourselves—is really extremely edifying." [7]

To our positive task, then, how may we convey God's message to this need? Here we recall four great means of communication, the word, the fellowship, the person and the deed.

1. In the beginning is the Word. Here we have in mind not the particular application of the word in personal counseling, but the word as it comes through the means of grace, the whole ministry of worship, including the sermon. That truly is group therapy. Eunice Tietjens has pictured this grace of empowered life:

I shall go down from this airy space, this swift white peace,
    this stinging exultation,
And time shall close about me, and my soul stir to the
    rhythm of the daily round.
Yet, having known, life will not press so close,
    And I shall always feel time ravel thin about me;
For once I stood
In the white windy presence of eternity. [8]

That is both diagnosis and cure. "Life will not press so close"—that is our predicament. Life does press close on us, like contracting walls. That is our cure—"I stood in the . . . presence of eternity."

The message, eternal but not remote, moves directly to man's chief concerns. T. S. Eliot writes, "To apprehend the point of intersection of the timeless with time, is an occupation for a saint." It is certainly the occupation for the preacher. To man's insecurity the gospel brings foundations; to his sense of aloneness, of separateness, it brings fellowship, it breaks the power of canceled sin and sets the prisoner free from his bonds; to his dejection, it brings hope. This communication is not the repetition of traditional words, for that has been, and may be, merely the dissection of "the flaccid tissues of long dead issues offensive to God and mankind." Gertrude Stein, strange as it may seem to those who know her only as the author of the immortal line, "A rose is a rose is a rose," was a wonderfully skillful medical student at Johns Hopkins University Medical School. She was almost awarded a degree because of her great competence in the dissection of corpses. It was denied because she had no interest whatever in the treatment of living patients. That same calamity may happen to preachers. They may retreat into the past and become adept in the dissection of corpses, and fail to have a consuming interest in the treatment of living, and suffering, patients. It is not the announcement of religious riddles, or theological puzzles. In his life of General Sherman, Lloyd Lewis records an incident in the battle of Shiloh where a teamster was struggling to drag a gun carriage up through the mire of a riverbank. A wandering evangelist seized on that strategic moment to do some evangelistic work. He said to the teamster in a sepulchral voice, "Do you know who died on a cross?" Without looking up, the teamster replied, "Don't ask me any riddles; I'm stuck in the mud." [9] A great many people are "stuck in the mud" these days, straining at loads beyond their immediate power. There is no lifting power in riddles or crossword puzzles.

Yet the gospel is no little all-purpose pill. The most immediate and only adequate help to all human need is that which, to a very common view, is the farthest away and intangible—God. The deepest need is the faith that underneath and above life is the transcendent God. Here we are indebted to many theologians who have stressed the need of the dimension of depth, transcending nature and transcending history, if life is to be sustained by a faith that reaches absolute bottom. The gospel is no "operation bootstrap." I shall never forget a homely yet conclusive documentation of that truth reported to me by a chaplain in World War I. He officiated at a mass burial of eleven men out of one company. A rainy day added to the gloom. The company was gathered at the grave pit. He said it was the dreariest day that ever dripped from the skies. He read the service; it was all correct and all lifeless. Just as they were about to leave, a little red-haired cook from Arkansas began to sing, "There's a Land That is Fairer than Day." That was just a living footnote to a theological dogma, "If Christ be not risen from the dead, then is our faith vain." Hope is vain, life is vain, without the help in ages past, the hope, the shelter—

Sufficient is thine arm alone
And our defense is sure.

Central in that word is this: "God so loved." We must not forget—what is easy to forget when we hear so much talk about "the worth of man"—that "the worth of man" is a theological dogma. Without the dogma of the love of God it has no invisible means of support. Great words pass by us incessantly, such as "the sacredness of personality" and that of William Faulkner in his impressive speech accepting the Nobel Prize, "Man is Immortal." It is well to play the part of a military sentry and challenge them with a "Halt, who goes there?" For those are loaded words: "sacredness" and "immortality." Loaded with the unacknowledged dependence on God's revelation in Christ. Without that they are mere parasites.

This is the ultimate resource which comes to a score of specific lacks. Go back in our thought to the expression quoted earlier, "Non-entity cards." The gift of God is an "identity card," a name, an identity in his love. "I will give Him a new name." That is the supreme gift when we live so much in a world of numbers, security numbers, draft numbers, tax numbers. The baby, new to earth and sky, born in a hospital, gets a number before he takes his second breath.

Peter Viereck has pictured this ultimate need:

> . . . Men are filed in their own filing system
> With frayed manilla folders for their souls,
> once labelled GOD'S OWN IMAGE: USE WITH CARE
> But now reclassified as OBSOLETE.[10]

The label is not obsolete. It is eternal. But there are so many forces tending to make it seem obsolete. When Bunyan's Pilgrim went into deadly battle with the great Apollyon, the giant gave a defiant cry, "Here will I spill thy soul." There are today so many powers which say, "Here will I spill thy soul," taking away the sense of personal significance and permanence. To restore that lifesaving sense of the value of the soul, our major task must be to make God real, to help people see daily life under the aspect of eternity, to bring into life a sacramental value. That means conveying the reality of God's search for man. That was a penetrating word spoken by a man who was rescued after days at sea in a rubber boat. He said, "My only hope was that I knew I was being sought." That spreads from the center of our gospel to the farthest fringes of the world. A shepherd had a hundred sheep. A woman had ten coins. A man had two sons. The seeking God!

This central faith reaches into one of our prevailing moods today, the sense of insecurity. Indeed, we seem as a people to have receded to what psychologists tell us are a baby's only two fears, the loss of security and a loud noise. We fear falling from our economic level and we fear a loud noise, an atomic crash. So deeply ingrained is this fear, that a current mark even of youth is not so much the traditional one of adventure or rebellion, but a premature grasp at security. There is the jittery feeling of insecurity of various sorts, economic, national and spiritual insecurity. Anxiety and fear are different states of mind. But they have all been lumped together under the heading of "An Age of Anxiety." The spiritual effects are much the same—flurry, fluster and fidgets. This mood is not the normal anxiety of every responsible person or the saving fear of many things that ought to be feared. It is more of a neurotic anxiety, being hagridden by vague apprehensions and dreads. Of course, anxiety is not all a liability. Men are not the lower animals. You never heard of a clam with a nervous break-down. There is nothing to break down. Man can say, "With a great price obtained I this freedom," this sensitive nervous system—at the price of pain and mental turmoil. It is worth far more than the price.

To this far-stretching mood we must bring again, as per-suasively as with God's help we can, the old command of Jesus, "Fear not, little flock."

Ours is not the first age of anxiety. The gospel was en-acted in one. The man who in the first century wrote, "Never be anxious," was speaking to an age of great anxiety. It had both the dreads we know, and many terrifying ones we no longer face. The condition we face is old, as the cure for it is old.

Inevitably, people turn, often frantically, to quack reme-dies. Some try to drown their worries in an alcoholic sea. Others try busyness as an anaesthetic. Others try to forget their anxieties by remembering their good fortunes, which turns out to be much like telling a man with a badly crushed finger to think of the nine good ones. It is like trying to cure an inward ill with court plaster.

It is a truism, but so is gravitation, that in a God of love is the only remedy for insecurity. Of course, economic in-security lays upon the Christian the compulsion to work to change the conditions which blight so many lives, so that cruel privation and the shackling of potentialities may not be the fate of millions of God's children. But deeper than that is security in God, where thieves do not break in or steal or moth corrupts. In Christian faith we replace an ignoble fear—fear of things that harm or kill the body, by a noble fear, fear of the things that kill the soul. "Fear not their fears." We quoted just now a fragment of a sentence, "Never be anxious." Finish the sentence and we have the victorious alternative to insecurity. "*But* in everything by prayer and supplication with thanksgiving let your requests be made known to God. And the peace of God, which passes all understanding, will keep your hearts and minds in Christ Jesus." The poet's words are just a paraphrase of that, "a central peace, subsisting at the heart of endless agitation." Life is redeemed from paralyzing agitation when the values that we have in God are greater than the threat to any other values. The world is not a marble which has slipped out of God's pocket, but a round globe which he loves, in his hands.

An inseparable part of our message is the victory over anxiety by the recentering of life, lifting it out of prison of self-interest into dedication patterned after the Great Model, "Not my will, but thine be done."

The gospel message, further, includes redemption from defeat. Take that prayer from the Psalms, "Let me never be put to confusion." [11] That means complete defeat. Our age knows a good deal about defeat, the life that is confounded. It needs the ancient trust, "Thou redeemest my soul from destruction"—from ultimate defeat. Our prayer is not that we may never be put to perplexity, nor to distress, but to defeat. St. Paul draws the distinction accurately. "We are afflicted in every way, but not crushed; perplexed, but not driven to despair; persecuted, but not forsaken; struck down, but not destroyed." [12] No ultimate defeat. The life in Christ may lose many battles, but win the campaign of life. It is a tragic symptom of our predicament that one of the key words of our world today is the word "split." We have split personalities, split families, split nations, split atoms. The gospel for a splitting world is that of Him "in whom all things hang together."

Again, the word we have received can overcome the ravages of the Big Lie. Today we usually reserve that term for the lies of Soviet Russia. And the Big Lie of communism is a whopper! But it is not confined to Russia. There is the Big Lie of a practical materialism all around us. It follows the same laws of propaganda that Russia does; make the lie big enough and yell it loudly enough and it will get itself believed. This Big Lie has gotten itself believed by multitudes—that life *does* consist of an abundance of things; that man *does* live by bread alone; that all things worth living *are* won by might and power and not by any unsubstantial spirit. T. S. Eliot has put part of the deadly lie into words, writing of people who "constantly try to escape from the darkness outside and within by dreaming of systems so perfect that no one will have to be good."

This lie is not new but old. Jesus spent a large part of his time refuting it. It appears in the penetrating words of Tertullian, in which he wrote of "men already civilized and under the illusions of their very culture." True of Rome in the third century, true of America in the twentieth! What a theme for the preacher, the illusions of our culture! And what an enemy to fight and strip of its deadly weapons. The illusion of one of its prophets, that "the business of America is business"; the illusion of the rich fool, as we often practice it, who gave all his attention to problems of production and not any to distribution; he was called a fool, you remember; the term still applies; the illusion that meat is more than life, and raiment more than body; the

illusion that spiritual diseases can be cured by material
remedies. In recent years we have had many striking por-
trayals of the truth that man cannot live on illusions. That
truth became flesh and walked on the stage in Tennessee
Williams' *Streetcar Named Desire*, in O'Neill's *The Ice-
man Cometh*, in Miller's *Death of a Salesman*. The Big Lie
must be overcome by the truth that makes men free.

At the heart of the Word we have received is the reality
of sin and the gift of God in forgiveness. This spreads so
widely into the whole human entanglement that here it can
be only affirmed as a first requirement if that word is to be
truly shared. It is fairly easy to cry out "repent!" It is so
difficult to bring the conviction of sin to people who are
doing pretty well as it is, thank you. Many outside and in-
side the churches will ask in genuine astonishment, "How
could there be anything wrong, any sin, if you must use that
word, with a way of life that has done so well by us?"
Another current difficulty in bringing the conviction of sin
is that often a superdetective is needed to trace the social
ramifications of sin. There is truth in the observation that
you can make a play out of one man robbing another man;
but not out of one man robbing a million men, still less
out of his robbing them unconsciously. Sin in these days
includes the sin of communal responsibility. "I never cut
my neighbor's throat—my neighbor's gold I never stole"—I
merely stood by, consenting; perhaps on occasion holding
the clothes of the active participants. Many people have
taken part in slow murder who never handled any lethal
weapon other than the scissors with which they cut cou-
pons. The sin that we do by two and two, and two million

by two million is shared guilt that must be faced one by one.

That is only part of the Word. The whole Word stands, "If we confess our sins, he is faithful and just to forgive us our sins, and to cleanse us from all unrighteousness" (A. V.). It is fascinating to meditate on the relation of religion to memory. Memory can be both hell and heaven. In dealing with sin, we can forget only by remembering. If men are ever to say "forgetting the things that are behind," that is, the shameful things, the sinful things, "the remembrance of them is grievous unto us," it is only by remembering the gift of the forgiveness of God in Christ. That received forgiveness is a never-absent need. Only that can truly restore the soul. So our only sufficiency is that through us the Holy Spirit may take this thing of Christ, forgiveness, and bring it unto people.

Finally, as far as the communication by the Word is concerned, we are the messengers of hope in a world darkened by increasing hopelessness. In a day when it has grown quite common to regard any kind of hope as romantic sentimentalism, it is well to recall words imbedded in the New Testament, "Now the God of hope fill you with all joy and peace in believing, that ye may abound in hope" (A. V.). To a different group, who from a different standpoint say with an unconcealed petulance, "Why bother with eschatology? Let's get on with the business of the Kingdom of God," to them we may answer, "There will be no business of the Kingdom of God without hope."

One element of that hope, of course, is the Christian hope of eternal life. Strange that it should be necessary to communicate that primary part of the Christian message to Christians. But the hope burns dim in the lives of many within the Church. <u>The first heralds of the gospel went out preaching Jesus and the Resurrection. But today, many, instead of being radiant witnesses of the resurrection, seem to have joined the secret service.</u> They keep it quiet. They end where the gospel of Mark ends, with the words, "They said nothing to any one, for they were afraid." Yet if Christ be not risen from the dead, Christianity has nothing to say with any power in the greatest crises of life. There is a memorable line in Masefield's *The Widow in the Bye Street* on the hope of eternal life, "A rest for broken things too broke to mend." Every week the preacher meets "broken things too broke to mend" in this world. If he cannot convey the hope of the mending of hopelessly broken things, he has nothing convincing to say.

For the struggle in this world against evil, so frightening and powerful, there is hope in the immeasurable resources of God. In the words traced on the walls of a dark catacomb in Rome, in a day incredibly dark, "His Kingdom is an everlasting Kingdom." It is the reasonable hope that God does not get to the end of his rope. Redemptive power has been released in Christ, power that does not diminish or vanish. This hope is not to be identified with the success of any particular program or distorted into any particular theory of social progress. We cannot picture any form of the ultimate victory of God. But we have the hope enshrined in the hymn,

> O God our help in ages past
> Our hope for years to come.

God is the Lord of the past and will be the Lord of the

future. So in the faith in that Lord of the future we can become fellow workers with him. When we sing with our hearts and minds as well as with our voices,

> From age to age the same
> And he must win the battle,

we are in the main stream of Christian tradition. The core of that hope is that God will act redeemingly in his world. The false hopes of so many in our own day compel us to proclaim incessantly, "Hope thou in God, and not in the many futile trusts." There is a striking resemblance between our age and that in which Jesus lived, in that both were ages of great messianic expectation. It is no exaggeration to say that this present time is one of intense messianic expectation. But like men of Jesus' time, many are looking for the wrong messiah. For multitudes among us there is no vision of a City of God coming down from the skies, such as appeared to the author of the book of Revelation. They have a vision of a vast conjuring trick coming up from the earth, from the mines and the factories—a paradise of chromium and ceramics, egg-shaped automobiles and layer-cake houses, skyscrapers made of glass, and clothing made of soybeans. They do not need a Day of the Lord; the General Motors will take care of all that! What a trade, God for gadgets, the reign of God for a salesman's paradise! We must recapture the expectation, "My expectation is from God."

I am one of many who look with deep distress on the efforts of some, many of them on the continent of Europe, who seek to channel the whole Christian hope into the narrow form of some sort of millennialism, the Second Coming of Christ, or the final "coming of Christ in glory."

That form is too small to encompass the whole meaning of the God of hope. We have seen, too often, that the effect of that is to cut the nerve of Christian effort with the conclusion that there is nothing we can do but passively wait for the final windup. For them the call is not to fight the good fight, putting on the whole armor of God, but to throw up the hands. For such a doctrine may spring not from faith but from despair.

2. Another and indispensable means of communicating the gospel is the Christian fellowship, the Church. That means, not so much an organization, as a company of people who express the reality of God who has laid hold on them. The whole gospel cannot be truly communicated except through people in relation to God and to one another. In the earliest days of Christianity many were attracted and won to the fellowship before they understood the Christian message.

It is often forgotten that the fellowship is a means of apprehending the gospel as well as embodying it and spreading it. St. Paul makes that vivid in his prayer, "that you . . . may have power to comprehend with all the saints what is the breadth and length and height and depth." [13] The saints, the fellowship, an instrument of comprehension! That is inevitable. A gospel of love cannot be realized in isolation, only in fellowship.

During World War II a strange item appeared in an English newspaper in a report of a concert. It read, "Miss Bessie Smith whistled the Fifth Symphony." I have no doubt that Bessie was an accomplished whistler. But she did *not* whistle the Fifth Symphony. No one ever did. It is not a solo but a symphony. It cannot be rendered by any soloist; only by an orchestra. Christianity is not a solo; it is a symphony. It can only be rendered by a fellowship, by orchestrated, blended lives. The divine love is mediated through a fellowship. A voice crying in the wilderness is not enough. A demonstration by linked lives is needed if the real nature of the gospel is to be made completely clear. It is glowingly expressed by the Theological Commission on Faith and Order:

The missionary in India can only convey to individuals the message, if we can point to a community of believers in whom this gospel is made actual. It is the forgiven and forgiving community of those who have received the adoption of sons which must mediate to the Hindu the Christian meaning of forgiveness. The more it is realized that the deepest Christian experiences are experiences of and within a fellowship, it becomes plain that the Church as the fellowship of the Holy Spirit plays a vital part in the transmission of the gospel to the world by the quality of its life.[14]

There is a beautiful and accurate simile of Brunner's "The Church exists by mission, as fire exists by burning." When the fire dies it is no longer a church. It meets the fate that has overtaken Salem, Illinois, called "The town that became a museum." So there can be a church that becomes a museum. We can go on a conducted tour around it. There is the creed in a glass case; there are the records in a safe. There are the mummies, once alive. And there will be no communication.

Within the church there is communication in the sacraments, the conveying that goes beyond words. That is a primary meaning of the word "communicant," we commune with God through the symbols, the divine drama of sacrifice, of forgiveness, of love, of fellowship.

3. Again, the gospel is communicated by the person who proclaims it and lives it. The question is raised for all of us for all time, in II Peter. "What sort of persons ought you to be in lives of holiness and godliness, waiting for and hastening the coming of the day of God . . . !" [15] We must be men through whose lives God shines. The gospel is communicated by personal experience of God in Christ, and the authority which issues from that. God set the pattern, "The word became flesh." I imagine that the word spoken by Dr. Robert Oppenheimer will find a permanent place in the anthologies of Christian devotion. He said, "The best way to send an idea is to wrap it up in a person." That was what God did in the Incarnation. That is what the messenger of God must do in an infinitely less degree but truly. The message must be wrapped up in his person. Only so can it be fully carried with compulsion. Spoken and printed words are faint when compared to the truth embodied in a person. Lowell has suggested this.

> Why I'd give more for one live bobolink
> Than a square mile of larks in printer's ink.

An experiment will underline this. I am convinced if I asked any one of you suddenly to recall five sermons you have listened to, you would be hard put to answer. But if I should ask you to name five persons through whom God has put his hand on your life, you would not hesitate a moment.

4. Finally, we communicate as persons and as a church by the Christian deed. There again, God set the pattern. "God so loved that he gave." We get the sequence in the story of the crucifixion. "Now when Jesus had finished all

2.2.019

these sayings"—what then? What came after the sayings? After the words, the *deed*. He went on to the cross. Never man spake like this man, but words were not enough to reveal the love of God. He was lifted up, and the act of the cross drew all men unto him. After our words, singly and together as a church, if the word is to be conveyed there must be the deed, the demonstration and validation by the action. All too often when we have finished our sayings, we pronounce "Amen," and it is all over. That is all there is. But after the sayings there must be the deed. The world is always waiting for the authentic signature of the thing done. It is the deed which gets us into trouble. But it is the deed through which God can be seen, even by those of dim vision. All over the world unconvinced multitudes are waiting for the courageous deed of love of sacrifice. Our resolutions have been glorious, a long list of eloquent phrases. But a Christianity without the enacting clause of action is just what St. Paul called it, "sounding brass."

IV

He Opened the Book

"HE opened the book and found the place." These words in the fourth chapter of Luke record the beginning of Jesus' ministry in Nazareth. In this first record of his spoken words, preaching began with opening the book and finding in it the word supremely fitting to the occasion. As it was in the beginning, it is now. That is one beginning, certainly, of every pulpit ministry, to communicate the truth in God's revelation in the Bible, to open it at the right place and time, so that the timeless truth may leap the centuries and be a part of our time, and a force in it. When Jesus opened the book of scripture, he did not merely restate the word, he re-created it. "This day is the scripture fulfilled in your ears." Ours, too, must be a ministry of re-creation of the words of scripture for present need.

To urge ministers to preach from the Bible is the reiteration of an axiom too obvious to be endured. It sounds like saying in the hushed accents of solemnity that it is well to keep your minds open to the possibility that two and two might make four.

Yet there are many things in the preacher's situation which make worth while the reiteration of so obvious a theme as the Bible as the unrivaled source of preaching.

One reason is that the preacher *has* to preach. We say

that we *want* to preach, but it is also true that we *have* to. Sometimes we can even say, "Woe is me, that I have to preach!" Out there ahead is next Sunday's sermon. In the words of Stevenson, "I have a little shadow that goes in and out with me." It is the shadow of next Sunday's sermon. And sometimes we can add in a low moan,

> And my soul from out that shadow
> Shall be lifted nevermore.

Bernard Shaw has made the life of a parish minister vivid. When he gave up the post of being drama critic on a London weekly paper, he protested against the deadline which had confronted him every seven days. He likened himself to a man fighting a windmill. He said, "I have hardly time to stagger to my feet from the knock down blow of one sail, when the next one strikes me down." That is the preacher's biography in a few words. The preacher fights the recurring deadline of a windmill for a lifetime.

So there is a continuing interest on the part of all of us in anything that may give new relationship to the basic truths of the gospel or a new framework which can be filled with the content of Christian truth.

There is no need to recommend Bible preaching to preachers. It is the only thing that keeps its freshness. The longer one is in the preaching ministry, the higher rating, I think, he puts on the Bible. The 13th chapter of I Corinthians has much to do with preaching as well as with Christian living. Listen to it:

> As for prophecy, it will pass away.

Isn't that true? We talk about the prophetic ministry, and one must have it, if he has any right to stand in a

Christian pulpit. But a congregation gets to know our witness on contemporary social and economic and intellectual questions. Man cannot live on an exclusive diet of the United Nations or atomic control. By the time you give your seventh sermon of the season on these things, the congregation gets a general idea of your stand on these issues.

As for tongues, they will cease.

That is oratory, the witchery of the tongue. I do not have it, so naturally I deplore it, as I deplore everything I do not have as being unimportant! Eloquence is important and a gift that has been greatly used in Christian history.

Yet for a congregation it ceases as an awakening instrument. Oratory is no substitution for fresh content. Preaching is like marriage in that respect. You may be married to the most beautiful girl in the world, beautiful, lovely; yet there comes a time—and it need not be ten years after the honeymoon—when you look across the table and say, "Yes, I know, you are beautiful and lovely, but what are we having for breakfast this morning?" There comes a time when the most wonderful golden hair and deep blue eyes are no substitute for bacon and eggs and a good cup of coffee. That is true of a congregation. They can look up at their preacher and say, "Yes, we know your golden voice, your gift of tongues—but what are we having for breakfast this Sunday morning?"

As for knowledge, it will pass away.

That means information. There is an essential educational function of preaching, but if it is mere knowledge, it passes away in its power to touch men to the quick and make them ask, "What shall we do?"

Now abideth prophecy, tongues and knowledge, and the greatest of these is the Bible.

It has a whole range of truth made fresh in a hundred lives and situations, capable of entangling the mind in a web of interest.

There is another reason for preaching that comes from the Bible—our need for authority. Dr. Gordon Poteat has written of this very pertinently:

> Up-to-date topical preaching, while timely, may lack the element of timelessness. It is too easily detached from Christian traditions, and thus cut off from any deep roots. Apart from this connection with the past, it may be questioned whether preaching, in any Christian meaning of the term, would persist. Another weakness in topical preaching is the tendency to monotony in the handling of the themes. When the preacher approaches his sermons primarily from the problem angle, he does not preach very long before he has compassed most of the possible themes. . . .
>
> The weakness of tradition detached, non-Biblical preaching is felt by many. The people in the pews seem to want something more, something different from what they get in editorials. . . . For many preachers with sensitive consciences it has become more and more difficult to ascend their pulpits "on their own." They realize that the expectation of the people exceeds that meager fare.[1]

To do justice to Dr. Poteat, we ought to go on to give his conception of fruitful Biblical preaching, which is that we do not preach ourselves, nor the Bible in itself, but "Christ Jesus as Lord." And that the Bible is the primary source of preaching only because it is the source of our knowledge of Jesus Christ; and that a return to Biblical preaching does not involve a rejection of the problems of contemporary life, either individual or social, but demands dealing with such problems in the light of the teaching of Jesus.

Without the Bible, the preacher is truly a displaced person, a refugee from his home country. He is, like so many people in our day *déraciné*, cut off from their roots, from the past of their town and country. Preaching needs deep Biblical roots if it is to combat the vicious contemporaneousness which blights so much thinking and feeling. We are in a generation in which real wisdom seems to require a temporary date line.

> The little front wave dashed upon the beach,
> And frothed there, wildly elated.
> "I am the tide," said the little front wave,
> "And the waves before me are dated." [2]

There is plenty of "front wave froth" around us. It splashes in every direction. To meet it the preacher needs the timeless dimensions of the Bible, deeper than a news broadcast or a psychological lecture, the dimensions both of man and his sin and of the grace of God.

Now, of course, there is danger in the study of the Bible as a source of sermon ideas. There is the danger of prostituting the Word of God into a mere instrument, something out of which the preacher may get a homiletical pound of flesh. The Bible is an instrument, but for a larger end than that of the contriving of sermons. It is an instrument in the revelation of God.

There is a striking passage in Osbert Sitwell's biography which bears on this. He is writing about his father, a constant visitor to art galleries. He writes,

My father sought only for decorative themes, and would say, after contemplating a great picture by Raphael or Botticelli, or a carving by Michael Angelo, "I am afraid it gives me nothing," as if to help him design a spoon or the leg of a chair had been the sole aim of the genius at whose work he had been looking.[3]

The chief aim of the spiritual geniuses whose work we have in the Bible was not to furnish texts or ideas for sermons, but to reveal God and his will.

One first indispensable equipment for communicating the truth in the Bible is a strong sense of the romance of exegesis. The word "romance" may seem to be a strange one to be coupled with exegesis. Scholarly exegesis has not been ordinarily regarded as a field for romance. But sound exegesis, so far from being a merely scholarly or scientific undertaking, can be a thrilling adventure in discovery. It sheds its ray into these great questions, using all the light and clues it can bring together, "What actually happened?" "What did these words mean as the writer used them?" In that it is a part of the high romance of history. One of the most readable of modern historians, George M. Trevelyan, has thus portrayed it,

How wonderful a thing it is to look back into the past as it actually was, to get a glimpse through the curtain of old night into some brilliantly lighted scene of living men and women, not mere creatures of fiction and imagination, but warm blooded realities, even as we are.[4]

That is what a dedicated and conscientious skill in exegesis gives, a sense of living people and living ideas. As brought to the book of Acts and Paul's Epistles, for instance, it helps us to step backward into another time and catch a vision of people making their way cautiously down dark streets to a little house, while the whisper goes around, "We have a letter from Paul." Pity the preacher who does

not know the zest of a careful exegesis. He has missed part
of his heritage. For it has some of the suspense of a detective story. It is a great detective story, the following of clues
into the mystery of the earliest proclaiming and reception
of the gospel.

Even the tracking down of early manuscripts has been
one of the world's greatest detective stories. Sherlock
Holmes never had an adventure to compare to that of
Constantin Tischendorf in the remote monastery of St.
Catherine on Mt. Sinai. He was a teacher in Leipzig who
set forth to find, if possible, early manuscripts of the New
Testament in monastaries and tombs of the Near East. On
the first evening of his arrival at the monastery while search-
ing out the building, his eye fell on a fuel bucket near a
fireplace. Looking over molded manuscript fragments which
were of no value he suddenly observed several pages written
in Greek uncials. He knew what it was. He wrote later, "At
that moment the world turned upside down in my head
and I saw all the colors of the rainbow." The forty-three
pages which he found belonged to what later became
known as the Codex Sinaiticus, one of the oldest known
manuscripts of the New Testament. It took fifteen years to
complete the search.

The same stirring adventure is to be found in the exegesis
of the scriptures, the thrill of realizing that these people
actually lived and this is how and what they thought and
did. Without a dedication to scholarly work, the preacher
will not fulfill his task as a communicator of the word. For
only in such study can he repossess the past. Preaching in
one dimension will not suffice for a historical religion. The
preacher who lacks the sense of history and reverence for

historical truth, as represented by exegesis, will merit the judgment in Charles Lamb's words,

> 'Tis man's worst deed,
> To let the things that have been run to waste,
> And in the unmeaning present sink the past.

Preaching that roots in the Bible is the only kind that may hope to compass the *wholeness* of the revelation of God. We know in part only and we see in part. "For our knowledge is imperfect and our prophecy is imperfect." [5] Only when the perfect comes in the full-circle revelation in the word will "the imperfect pass away." Each of us "on his own" is bound to be fractional in vision and emphasis. The pit which yawns in front of us as preachers is well described in a musical comment by Bernard Shaw. Of the performance of a violinist, he wrote, "At his first appearance he tried over the Kreutzer Sonata, and did not seem to think much of it, though here and there a passage struck him as rather good." Let that sink in, the selective attitude. "Parts of it were rather good." There, but for the grace of God in the revealed word, go all of us!

In this respect there is always the danger of using a "mutilated" Bible. Not, certainly, in the sense that Thomas Jefferson edited and published a mutilated Bible. He abridged the New Testament for the use of the Indians, "unembarrassed by matters of fact and faith beyond their comprehension." It consisted of the life story and ethical teachings of Jesus, with all supernatural features omitted. How delightfully "unembarrassed!" Yet such a mutilated Bible is often put out for the use of people with a higher cultural level than the Indians of colonial times. A few years ago there was one complacently entitled *A Bible for the Liberal*. Concerning it one reviewer wrote approvingly, "The editor is not concerned with doctrine. Only what constitutes to a better understanding of the meaning of life will be found in his pages." Beautifully simple! Obviously, the incarnation, crucifixion and resurrection of Jesus make no contribution to the better understanding of life!

The Christian preacher is in small danger of that sort of fatal mutilation. But everyone is in danger of ill-proportioned selection due to his fractional interests and tastes. The preacher can easily become the prisoner of his own temperament and limitations. Only in the whole range of the Bible can he get into the length and the breadth and height and depth of the revelation of the love of God.

There is always an inexorable demand for honesty in the use and interpretation of the Bible. For we are confronted steadily with the peril of first reading into the scripture our own conceptions and conclusions, and then bringing them out of the word. It is the old rabbit trick of the magician—first put the rabbit into the hat deftly, when no one is looking, and then bring it out, to the surprise and delight of the onlookers. It is a clever trick. But we are not called to be prestidigitators, but interpreters and heralds, rightly—that is, honestly—dividing the word of truth. It was a preacher, one of the greatest in the early Church, a master of exposition, Chrysostom, while many around him were quite carried away by the fashion of the time, the so-called "gnostic key" to the New Testament, who was cautious. He insisted on looking for the sense of the words in the context, and warned that every passage should be studied as a whole. There is timeless value in the warning.

One obvious power of the Bible for preaching ought never to be forgotten, though all too often it goes into low visibility. That is the moving force of dramatic narrative. Preaching needs drama desperately. Preaching needs drama to save itself from walking off into a philosophical wilderness, a sort of Sahara Desert of abstraction. There is much to remember in the schoolboy's definition of an abstract noun as "something which you can't see when you are looking at it." That is often true.

In thinking of drama, the first thing to be remembered, of course, is the truth which Dorothy Sayers has put so forcefully, that the Christian dogma is the drama. She writes, "A kind of pageant of sentiments and pale emotions has been substituted for the drama that is the Christian way. And the dogma is the drama." [6] Christianity did not come into the world on the editorial page but on the news page. The preacher is not a gushing geyser of good advice, but an announcer of good news.

But, in addition to that sense of the word "drama" there is the power of gripping narrative in which the Bible, both Old and New Testaments, abounds. To lose that is to trade our Biblical birthright for a very thin pottage. One of the preacher's great tasks, in dealing with the range of characters in the Bible, is to get them out of Statuary Hall. That room in the Capitol at Washington is one of the dreariest places in America. The visitor, it is true, is surrounded by a cloud of witnesses from American history. But they are all done in cold marble, and most of the statues are in rigid stuffed-shirt attitudes, some even in Roman togas, stiff and incredibly dead. Any statuary hall is an unalluring place, where life has been replaced by stone. The tremendous personalities of the Bible have often become mere conventional statues. The supreme tragedy is that even Jesus has become a statue, hastily venerated and passed by. That is not true when the characters in the Bible are allowed to walk on the screen of the imagination. If we stay close enough and long enough with the Bible narrative itself, we are better equipped to perform the old miracle of Eden, to breathe into the people in the Bible the breath of life, so that they become living souls.

This power of dramatic narrative is highlighted by the history of the oral transmission of much material now found in the gospels. It is impressive to remember that for many years much of the content of the gospels was carried in the memory of people. We do well to ask what kind of material stuck in the memory for years, as securely lodged as a fly in a spider's web. The answer is that it was largely material of two sorts—narratives, and short, short statements, often epigrammatic, easy to remember and repeat. Stories such as "A certain man had two sons," "The land of a rich man brought forth plentifully," and the sharp thrust of "He that loseth his life shall find it." The lesson from that, put very simply, is, "Go thou and do likewise."

There is also the asset of the poetry of the Bible, ideas and language which touch the secret places of the heart with a power that can never be matched by serviceable textbook prose. As a poet, Walter de la Mare, puts it, "Poetry no more keeps its meaning when turned into prose than a picture or sonata keeps its meaning in the little analyses they print in catalogs and programs. Kreisler or a symphony will not go into a program note."

One of the supreme opportunities and functions of

preaching is the creation of a bridge on which the truth disclosed in Palestine many centuries ago may be carried into the life and experiences of our time, and into the minds and hearts of the listening congregation. This is the high art of translation which the preacher must master. Consider two illustrations of that bridge building for the imagination. The first is from science.

One of the most effective demonstrations, all the more effective because wholly unintended, of what preaching from a Biblical narrative may be as a message to the contemporary world is found in a chapter in a book published two years ago, *One World or None,* written by atomic scientists. In the first chapter, Professor Phillip Morrison of Cornell, who worked on the atomic bomb at Los Alamos, New Mexico, describes his visit to Hiroshima to investigate the effects of the bomb. He is extremely eager to make the whole thing vivid to Americans, so after a short description of the devastation at Hiroshima he moves the whole catastrophe to New York. He writes:

The streets and buildings of Hiroshima are unfamiliar to Americans. Even from pictures of the damage, realization is abstract and remote. A clearer and truer understanding can be gained from thinking of the bomb as falling on a city which Americans know well. The diversity of the awful experience which I saw at Hiroshima, I shall project on an American target. . . .

Take that phrase—"project on an American target." That is one secret of effective preaching from the Bible. Professor Morrison imagines the bomb dropping in Gramercy Park in New York City. Then by exact measurements, one mile, two miles, etc., he shows just what would have happened in New York.

So, move the story into the familiar scene of American life. Many poets do substantially the same thing. The classic is in Francis Thompson's "O World Invisible We See Thee":

> But (When so sad thou canst not sadder)
> Cry, and upon thy so sore loss
> Shall shine the traffic of Jacob's ladder,
> Pitched between heaven and Charing Cross.[r]

And again:

> And Lo, Christ walking on the water
> Not of Gennesaret, but Thames.

So, also, William Blake:

> And did those feet in ancient times
> Walk upon England's mountain green?
> And was the Holy Lamb of God
> On England's pleasant pastures seen?

The answer to that question is, of course, "No." And yet, the poet moves the gospel powerfully to England.

As stressed earlier, there is the danger of illegitimately importing into the gospel narrative ideas and phraseology which do not belong there. Against that we must watch and pray, and strive till our last sermon has been preached. But there is just as great danger on the other hand, that of leaving the truth back in Palestine. We need the courage of the tightrope walker.

In writing of the presentation of Shakespeare in the theater, Margaret Webster, in her *Shakespeare without Tears*, had laid down a first rule that applies as closely to preaching as it does to drama. She says that it is highly important for the producer to know the theater in which Shakespeare was first presented, and the people for whom he wrote, the actors he had in mind, the conditions which hampered or liberated him, and the audiences which first saw Hamlet. But, she writes, such knowledge must not be sought as an end in itself. The producer must know even better the theater in which Shakespeare *must live now, if he is to live at all.* The italics are ours, for the truth deserves screaming italics. We must know the world and the audience in which Christ is to live now, if he is to live at all!

An amusing and even ludicrous anachronism of a small imaginative child points to this same truth. When young Robert Louis Stevenson was sick, an uncle offered a prize among his nephews for the best history of Moses. Louis dictated his entry, and drew illustrations showing the Israelites wearing top hats and smoking pipes, both of which his father did. He won the award.[8] Ridiculous! Israelites in top hats! Nevertheless, the child's drawings might well illumine the truth that the temptations and sins and struggles of the ancient Israelites were the same as those of the men in top hats in Edinburgh! That was on a much lower level but still had resemblance to the "anachronism" so often seen in the paintings of the Middle Ages, in which the people in Bible scenes were dressed in the clothes of the age in which the painter worked. The truth which was far off, in time and geography, was brought near.

The use of imagination, to carry truth across the chasm of the centuries, requires stern discipline. It is like the discipline demanded in the use of any high explosive. There must be the dedication to the truth, displacing any desire

for effect. Here is a contrast between the illegitimate and
legitimate use of the imagination in dealing with history.
The first is from Emil Ludwig, a good demonstration of
how not to do it:

> Bonaparte rides slowly across the desert sands to look upon
> the face of the Sphinx. . . . We can guess his thoughts. "Alex-
> ander stood here; Caesar stood here; they lived two thousand
> years after this image was sculptured, as I live two thousand
> years after them. Immeasurable empires, consecrated to the sun,
> extended around the Nile." [9]

Do not guess anybody's thoughts!

The second example is a restrained but effective use of
imagination as a first aid to the understanding of a historical
situation, in which the author does not guess thoughts but
portrays a comparable modern situation. It is from the
work of Dom Gregory Dix on the development of the
Christian communion service, *The Shape of the Liturgy.*
He paints a vivid impression of what being a Christian
meant for an ordinary middle-class citizen in Rome in the
age of the martyrs. He does it by moving the scene to contemporary England. The first word in this quotation is a
marvelous word for a preacher—*Suppose!*

> Suppose you were a grocer in Brindesbury, a tradesman in a
> small way of business, as so many of the early Christians were.
> Week by week at half past four or five on Sunday morning an
> ordinary working day in pagan Rome. Before people were
> stirring you would set out in the silent streets, with something
> in your pocket looking very like what we should call a bun or a
> scone. At the end of your walk you would slip in through the
> mews at the back of one of the big houses near Hyde Park,
> owned by a wealthy Christian woman. There, in her big draw-
> ing room, looking just as it did every day, you would find the

"church" assembling—socially a very mixed gathering indeed. A man would look keenly at you as you went in . . . but he knows you and smiles and says something. Indeed you loosely know one another well, you exchange greetings and nod and smile. People who are jointly risking at least penal servitude for life, by what they are doing, generally make certain that they know their associates. At the other end of the drawing room, sitting in the best arm chair, is an elderly man, a gentleman by his clothes, but nothing out of the ordinary—the bishop of London. On either side of him is standing another man. On chairs in a semi-circle, looking very obviously like what they are —a committee—sit the presbyters. In front of them is a small drawing-room table.

The author goes on to describe the eucharist. Then, still in terms of contemporary England, he goes on to describe a scene which happened again and again:

But perhaps it did not all end quite so easily. You might never walk back to Maida Vale again. Perhaps the bishop stopped to speak to some one on the front door step as he went out, and was recognized by a casual passer-by who set up a great shout of "Christian! Christian!" And before any one quite realized what was happening a small jostling crowd had collected from nowhere, a someone had thrown a brick through one of the windows . . . and there was a hubbub of jeers and yells, till a policeman arrives majestically, demanding, "Wot's all this 'ere?" "It's those . . . Christians again!" shouts someone, and the policeman gets out his notebook and looks severely at the bishop.

So in our modern analogy, fifteen Christians were hanged that afternoon at Wandsworth.[10]

That certainly looks like an honest and successful endeavor to convey what it meant to be a Christian in Rome in the days of persecution. Beyond that, it suggests a profound truth that the only way truly to capture "the feel" of New Testament times is to face the same experiences, both evangelistic and testing, things the men and women of the New Testament faced.

There must be a lifelong dedication to the study of the Bible. In this realm, he that putteth his hand to the plow and looks back is not worthy of the Kingdom of God. Again and again instances of devoted care in the field of the arts put the preacher to shame. Consider, for instance, the story of Charles de Tolnay. As a young student in 1921 he saw for the first time the glory of the ceiling of the Sistine Chapel. The sight moved him so deeply that he resolved to devote his life to the study of Michelangelo in the hope of presenting the master with a completeness and understanding never before given to an artist. That is just what he did over the years. Everything came under his eye and mind, every problem of the paintings and the artist; the whole vast realm of accumulated scholarship.[11] The massive result faces us with the question, "If the Sistine ceiling is worthy of such a life of devotion—and it was, emphatically—is not the theme of the paintings, God's revelation of Himself, worth much more consecration?"

This study must be actual study, and not the hurried use of the Bible as a possible means of finding a theme or text for a sermon. If read in that way, we do not really read the Bible at all. It is obvious that reading a book for one specific, limited purpose is not the same as reading it for its own inherent value. Thus, if a man is reading a book for the purpose of a review, he does not read it truly; he is preoccupied with the necessity of finding something to say. He is more concerned with himself than with the book in it-

self. Stephen Spender, the poet, has put this sharply out of
his own experience.

On looking back I see that often in reviewing a book, I was
too ready to take up certain points I agreed with or disagreed
with, and make them the subject of the review, instead of reviewing the book as a whole. If I read a book with the idea of
writing a review I approached it with a different attitude of
mind from when I read it out of simple curiosity. As a reviewer
I was, as it were, interrupting what the writer had to say, with
the pressure of my need to write a few hundred words, and this
had much the same effect as not listening to someone's remarks
because one is thinking how to answer them.[12]

That may be the preacher's snare, not to pay real attention,
because of the sermonic pressure "to write a few hundred
words." From that trap, Good Lord, deliver us!

One practical aspect of the necessity of the preacher's living with the Bible must not be overlooked. Go back in your
thought to the words quoted at the beginning of this chapter, in the narrative of Jesus in the synagogue at Caper-
naum, "He opened the book and found the place." Finding
the place is supremely important, and often the right place
cannot be found unless the preacher knows the whole Bible
intimately. Jesus knew exactly where in Isaiah was the fitting word for his purpose on the occasion. Often that fitting
word is missed because the preacher simply does not know
where it is and cannot find the place.

A pertinent, if amusing, instance of this is found in
Abraham Lincoln's remarkable knowledge of what is in the
Bible. In the summer of 1864, when it was dolefully said by
him, "There are no Lincoln men," a convention of mal-
contents and haters of Lincoln was called at Cleveland for

the purpose of preventing his election to the presidency.
Vast crowds were prophesied.

When a friend told him that instead of the thousands who
had been expected at Cleveland, only about four hundred had
been present, Lincoln was struck by the number. Reaching for
the Bible that lay handy on his desk, he thumbed through it to
I Samuel 22:2 and read, "And every one that was in distress,
and every one that was in debt, and every one that was discon-
tented, gathered themselves unto him; and he became a captain
over them: and there were with him about four hundred
men." [13]

On a higher level there is a word that has gone into history. It is the word of Thomas Chalmers, Moderator of the
Scottish Church, who was presiding at a session in which
many of the stock arguments against foreign missions were
trotted out. In his anger he called, "Rax me that Bible!"
And when someone "raxed" him a Bible, he "opened the
book and found the place" where the universal nature of
the love of God and the missionary obligation of the
Church were set forth compellingly. He knew the book!

The preacher must live with the Bible so that if the
world came down in ruins tomorrow it would find him
working on some portion of scripture; not for Sunday, but
because it is a lifelong process with him, passing in review
before his mind the whole truth of the Bible. You have
probably already found that the most vital sermons that
you ever had were not those that were prepared for special
occasions, but were those that you glimpsed when you were
reading the Bible and had no need to be preparing for anything in particular. The mind works when it doesn't have
to, and often when compelled it won't work at all. So that

when the occasion arises you must get something that you've "seen the other day." I remember up in Vermont a crowd of children on a "treasure hunt." It was one of these treasure hunts where people are sent out to get a list of impossible things and bring them back. One requirement was to bring back a snake. A snake is a hard thing to meet when you are looking for one. And nearly all the teams—there were a dozen of them—found what they had to bring back, but only one couple brought back a snake. Sure enough it was a dead one, but it was a snake. The other children were very jealous. They asked one winner, "How on earth did you happen to find a snake?" He said, "I saw it yesterday." Now the advice to the preacher is this: See your snakes yesterday! Have a yesterday in which you have lived with the Bible!

The pertinence of the Bible is both amazing and inexhaustible. An important conversation was once held between Humpty Dumpty and Alice, as recorded in *Alice through the Looking Glass*. Humpty Dumpty is saying,

"The King has promised me—with his very own mouth—to—to—"

"To send all his horses and all his men," Alice interrupted rather unwisely.

"Now I declare, that's too bad!" Humpty Dumpty cried, breaking into a sudden passion. "You've been listening at doors —behind trees—and down chimneys—or you couldn't have known it!"

"I haven't, indeed," Alice said very gently. "It's in a book."

That is the wonder of a book. It is the wonder of the Book! So much of the wonder of God and man, of life and death, of time and eternity is in this Book! It is one of the amazements of history that from this collection of writings which has been more continuously and extensively studied than any other body of writing in the world, there appear "bright shoots of everlastingness," as fresh as a garden in spring.

Sometimes the sharp timeliness of the Bible passage comes from a picture for the imagination, rather than from exegesis, yet a picture which does not distort the words or read into them a foreign meaning. Take, for instance, the words in the second verse of the first chapter of Genesis, describing the void before creation, "the earth was without form, and void; and darkness was upon the face of the deep." What a picture of our world today—chaos awaiting a creation! Our earth is without form, dying of multiplicity because it does not recognize its unity, the need for the Spirit of God to move on the face of the waste. Very different in nature, but of great timeliness, is the foundation of democracy in the Old Testament. It was the Hebrew tradition that first insisted that all men were equal in the sight of God. Professor Irwin Edman regards Samuel as the first democrat, and the "Book of the Covenant the first instance of social contract." There is iron and fire in the prophets of the Old Testament to oppose a fashionable evil of our time, a sweet and sentimental religion which turns inward exclusively, and turns away from the evils which ride roughshod over people. We need what is found strongly in the Old Testament, the devastating deflation of our contemporary confidence in achievement. Consider also the parallel between the problem of our churches today and that of the exile as we find it depicted in Ezekiel and the latter part of Isaiah. It is the problem of the preservation of our religion in an alien culture. Our problems in

what has been called "a post-Christian age," or in Toyn-
bee's word, an "ex-Christian age" is like that of the exiles in
Babylon. Then there is the theme all through the Bible,
the need and difficulty of maintaining the inner life in a
civilization so largely quantitative.

There is the need for an ancient wisdom for a lifetime
rather than a new prudence for every hour. Take the old
question that is always new, the question of war—is there a
word that goes nearer to the whole issue than this old question, "Shall I give the fruit of my body for the sin of my
soul?" Is that not an exact description of war? Our sins of
omission today bring the human sacrifices of tomorrow.
Think of that wonderful picture of Nehemiah looking out
over devastated Jerusalem. What a picture that is of a
ruined civilization waiting to be built around us!

Here is one, old as the hills: "So they took Dagon and
put him back in his place." [14] The old god, the old idol
which in a hundred places in our world is being set up in
its place! The old idols of nationalism, and the god of
profits! I think of that text in Mark where a little girl had
died and they came to Jesus and they said to him, "Lay
thine hands upon her and she will live." [15] That may be
taken as a picture of the tremendous truth that anything
that Jesus is allowed to lay his hands upon lives. He can lay
his hands on the sex instinct and it can live. He can lay his
hands on an economic system and make it live.

Think how this word from Micah fits into a dominant
mood in America, "And you shall bow down no more to
the work of your hands." Or this text, quaint-looking but
with profound importance today, "They do not know how
to blush." Bring an answer to the question in II Peter,

"What sort of persons ought you to be in lives of holiness and godliness, waiting for and hastening the coming of the day of God." [16] How clearly it images the danger of being ordinary in extraordinary times! The power of many such a text is partly in the fact that the congregation does not know that the text is loaded until the preacher pulls the trigger!

The deepest need of all which the Bible meets is glimpsed in a wistful word in a magazine article, in which the author asks about people, "What are they waiting for in the sermon in print or from the platform? Perhaps for precisely what they no longer get, the note of revelation, the accent of ecstasy, the guiding principle, the keystone of their lives." The preacher must bring that note of revelation and accent of ecstasy. If he is to do that, the Word of God must be his native country, the homeland of his mind. An English writer Helen Thomas, in her book *World without End*, writes feelingly of her native Wiltshire, "As my feet trod these ancient ways my heart was filled with joy to know that this Wiltshire country belonged to me and I to it with all its history and tradition, bareness and richness, toil and harvest, simplicity and mystery."

So the preacher must say, by the grace of God and his own dedicated study and experience, "This country belongs to me."

V

The Preacher as Craftsman

THE whole plot of this chapter could be given in one
sentence. It is this: The aim of preaching is not the
elucidation of a subject, but the transformation of a person.
When we have said that we must hurry on to add that all
through the Christian centuries a most effective instrument
in the transformation of a person has been the elucidation
of a subject. The first Christian sermon at Pentecost was
emphatically the elucidation of the subjects of Hebrew history and prophecy. It resulted in the transformation of
people.

Yet the purpose of the preacher is not to explain something but to persuade people to think, and to act, in a
certain way. One of the hardest tasks in any theological
seminary is to take students who are spending three years
in a world where, inevitably and rightly, the emphasis is on
explaining something, and persuade them that in a church
and congregation they are in a different world which demands a different goal and approach. The most wonderful
demonstration of that difference is in Jesus' conversation
with the woman at the well in Samaria, a sermon to one
person. There we see him, with love and skill, turning what
might have been an academic discussion of history and worship into a personal appeal and the conviction of sin. Our

task is to give to doctrine a moving presentation which goes beyond exposition into persuasion. The sermon must be judged operationally by its effect on the hearers.

This means the recognition that the sermon itself is merely secondary. It is an instrument. James Russell Lowell furnishes sure guidance here. He pictures his poetic Muse saying to him,

> The epic of a man rehearse
> Be something better than thy verse.

If we are not something *better* than our sermons, we are of all professions most miserable, for we are in a profession of *being*. In that respect churches in many periods have violated the Second Commandment, "Thou shalt not bow down to any graven image." They have often made an idol out of the sermon. We should always remember the partnership of Aaron and Moses. Aaron had the technique. He was a ready talker. But Moses had chosen for him the better part. He had something to say, imparted to him by God.

In the craftsmanship of the preacher first place must be given to one of the basic principles of much modern architecture, "form follows function." That applies all the way from a chair to a skyscraper. If it is a chair, why not make something to sit on, instead of a disguised featherbed? If a gymnasium is being built, why make a Gothic cathedral? The previous question is always, "What is the function of this talking?" A student years ago reported his consternation on finding in the pulpit where he was a supply preacher a little card on which was printed the question, "What are you trying to do with these people?" That upset him, for he was not really trying to do anything. He was just preaching. There is a parallel in the art of stage managing. The stage manager's work begins long before the first rehearsal. The first need is to get clearly in mind what the author is saying, and then to bring everything, voice, costume, scenery properties, to that one focal point. We are all familiar with the division of spoken and written words into three forms, the solid, liquid and gaseous. Dean Inge said that the solid is the form taken by books written by professors for or at each other. The gaseous, alas, needs no definition! We all know it. The liquid form gives more promise. When learning is held in solution, it may convey the invitation to people, "Ho everyone that thirsteth, come and drink!"

In preaching, as in all creative writing, the thing of first importance is not plots but people. A novelist gave good advice to a young writer when he wrote, "Do not rack your brain contriving plots. Get out among people. See them, hear them, study them." It is good advice to the preacher. If we do that, we will strive to bring scholarship to the point of need, just as we bring the resources of the past in electricity, Volta, Joseph Henry, Franklin, Edison, when we snap an electric switch to meet a particular need. We may well note that the commonly used phrase, "a preacher's preacher," may be double edged and terribly dangerous. It is like the other phrase, " a poet's poet," frequently given as a minor prize to a poet too precious to be human nature's daily food. Edmund Spencer was "a poet's poet" and achieved the notable distinction of becoming obsolete in his own lifetime. To be "a preacher's preacher" is a thin prize beside "The common people heard him gladly." One minister has told me that for years he kept this little parable in sight. It describes a man speaking to a man dying of thirst in the Sahara:

> Let us consider the properties of what we call water. Water is a colorless liquid which on being raised to a temperature of a hundred degrees Centigrade or two hundred and twelve degrees Fahrenheit, it becomes what is called vapour. If, however, on the other hand, the temperature is lowered to no degrees Centigrade, or thirty-two degrees Fahrenheit, lo, it is ice! In the final analysis it is discovered to consist of two portions of hydrogen to one of oxygen, hence arises the name H_2O.
>
> The thirsty man interrupts, "For the love of God, mister, a drink!"

The resources of the gospel must be brought to the existing situation. That is the kind of "existentialism" that the preacher most needs. Go back for a moment to the sermon mentioned a moment ago, that of Peter at Pentecost. It did bring the resources of history and theology to an existing situation. Recall it. It was aimed at a definite mark. Peter did not sail gracefully around in the upper air like a sea gull. His talk went to its mark like a bullet, that the Jesus who had been crucified had risen and was God's Messiah. It had the gospel in it. No one went away wondering what Peter had been talking about. What he said about Jesus was a jolt to most of his hearers, but it was not a blur. Also, the sermon reached them; "they were cut to the heart." The audience realized that the preacher was not indulging in vocal gymnastics or taking central breathing exercises in public. He wanted them to do something. The conclusion was specific. He did not end up in a verbal sunset, or with the first-century equivalent of "Well, it is nice to have seen you." He said, "Repent and be baptized." Many of them did so.

Recall another preacher. In one chapter, the 14th Chapter of Luke, there are recorded four separate occasions when Jesus saw the situation around him, and brought his word to that condition. The first was the occasion of a healing on the Sabbath. He felt the opposition, and brought the little comparison of the ox or the ass fallen into a well on the Sabbath. Again, when he was at dinner he "marked how they chose the places of honor," and to that greedy self-pushing he brought the crushing word, "Every one that exalts himself will be humbled." Again, when someone at the table went into the sentimental rhapsody "Blessed is he who shall eat bread in the Kingdom of God," he spoke directly to that and told the story of those who rejected the invitations and are rejected by God. When he saw multitudes following him he gave to them his tremendous sermon on counting the cost, "Whoever does not bear his own cross, cannot be my disciple."

Preaching which goes directly into a situation or observed need may be called, in the highest sense of the word, "journalistic preaching," moving into what is going on. Bernard Shaw was right, and not merely "smart," when he said that what did not originate as journalism has never endured as literature. When St. Paul got about two thirds of the way through his first letter to the Corinthians, he did not say to himself, "Now I will write a poem which will go down through the ages." He was trying to bring the spirit of love into the settlement of a church quarrel, and what we know as the thirteenth chapter of I Corinthians was an instrument of that particular endeavor. But some may ask, "How about the *Divine Comedy* and *Paradise Lost*. Were they journalistic?" Thank you for mentioning them! They are splendid examples. Both of them dealt with what were dominant interests and concerns of their generation, not of ours, but of theirs. Neither Dante nor Milton was consciously writing for immortality. They were bringing their own vision to their own time.

This focal point of a message in seen need will help the preacher to escape from one of the most dangerous illusions about his work. That illusion can be felt in the sigh which every preacher has made, "O that I had wings like a dove. Then I would fly away, and write some great sermons under the right conditions." Watch out! The dove is a deceptive bird. Don't trust him. You may flap your wings and fly away into peace, perfect peace, but you will also get far away from the unfailing source of real communication of God's truth to felt need. That source is in the complex and heavily loaded entanglement of people's lives.

Rudyard Kipling was not writing about preaching, but his observation on his four years in the United States goes right to the heart of this matter. He wrote,

> I had known a corner of the United States as a householder, which is the only way of getting at a country. Tourists may carry away impressions, but it is the seasonal detail of small things and doings, (such as putting up fly screens and stove-pipes, buying yeast cakes and being lectured by your neighbors) that bite into the lines of mental pictures.[1]

It is involvement in life which makes sermons bite into the mind and heart.

This demands more than depending on the false reliances that beckon seductively to the herald of the Word. Sometimes those allurements come in the form of labor-saving devices, which appeal to our taint of original sin. But more often they are reliances on tricks of one sort and another, devices which hold forth the promise of startling effect. That, of course, was Satan's temptation of Jesus. "Depend on tricks. Don't begin on the slow process of a sower going forth to sow. Bring in some magic." So, many have found the secret of preaching in some outward, superficial novelty. They are like the young artist who announced that he had discovered "the secret of Rembrandt." He had been examining the light in Rembrandt's "Night Watch" and discovered that "the secret was to paint in the cellar with no light except what comes in through a key hole." That is not too far removed from a preacher's devotion to what he calls "Gimmicks," some verbal twist, or some unusual pattern of ideas. He believes in salvation by novelty, not by the freshness of renewed experience. But the curiosity that no one ever thought of before is rarely worth thinking about. If man cannot live by bread alone, the preacher cannot live by tricks. One minister, in self-pity, said that to think that there are fifty-two Sundays in a year is enough to give a man heart failure. If he thinks of a year's preaching as calling for fifty-two brilliant ideas, he *ought* to have heart failure and be carried off. There is no salvation in a procession of novelties, but only in the realized and imparted passion for the great things of the gospel. "Gimmicks" are not the bread of life; they are more like a cunningly contrived pretzel. When a man depends on striking novelties, he will find whether he ever knows it himself that his mind has become like a child's bank—nothing but nickels and dimes will either go into it or come out of it.

In thinking of preaching that fails to convey the imperishable gospel, we might construct a little museum of sermonic models that were much used but are now obsolete and ought to be retired. They are frail reeds to lean on. One goes clear back to Robert Hall, who described the preaching of one of his contemporaries as being the "rocking horse sermon," with motion like a rocking horse which moves but does not go on, always charging but never advancing. Then there is what might fairly be called the mocking-bird sermon which, following a poet's description, "pours forth in unhesitating sequence, all the notes of the feathered choir." All the notes of someone else, either stolen or just imitated. Among the futilities "the Christmas tree sermon" has been popular, a lamentable collection of bright ornaments hung on a subject with no more vital relationship to it than the tinsel has to a Christmas tree. Some of the types of sermons which are inadequate in results have their point of weakness in words without sharp meaning, that result in "the Smörgåsbord Sermon." Like its namesake, it has little of everything and nothing very solid. The sentimentalist used to achieve a sermon fortunately quite obsolete now, but still heard. It was a "Confectioner's sermon," built like a wedding cake, a great airy structure with candy chateau, gardens of angelica, true lovers knots of sugar, and hearts of purest whipped cream. Sweet, but not much nourishment. Far more frequently heard is the procession of words deserving to be named "the Jericho Sermon." Some preachers follow the plan of Joshua's capture of Jericho. They seem to have implicit faith that if they march around the outside of a subject seven times, making a loud noise, the walls will fall down. They rarely do.

Our unending struggle is with words. There is no discharge in that war. Words are the speaker's ally. They may be his enemy and defeat his purpose. They may become a mere melody, a soothing sound. The danger is increased by the fact that many people, and, we might venture to add, particularly people in church, like to be massaged with words. As S. I. Hayakawa has observed, "They are interested only in the gentle inward massage that the sound of words gives them. Just as cats and dogs like to be stroked, so do some human beings like to be verbally stroked at fairly regular intervals." [2] That, of course, is as old as Ezekiel. "And, lo, thou art unto them as a very lovely song of one that hath a pleasant voice, and can play well on an instrument: for they hear thy words, but they do them not." [3] The love of "a lovely song" is always a prophet's hazard. He may develop a beautiful style in which, like a bee drowned in its own sweetness, his message is submerged.

A different danger lies in the development of a formal style from which familiar forceful words of common speech, which have the power to convey sense impressions, evoke memories and touch deep places of the heart, are missing. The birthright of common speech is traded for a pottage of polysyllables. Language has had most of the color bleached out of it. William Butler Yeats has pictured this calamity memorably. It is in a little poem entitled "The Stolen Child." He described a child kidnaped from earth by fairies and carried away to an ethereal cloud-land heaven, leaving all his natural earthly speech and scenes behind him.

> Away with us he's going,
> The solemn-eyed.
> He'll hear no more the lowing
> Of calves on the warm hillside,

Or the kettle on the hob
Sing peace into his breast,
Or see the brown mice bob
Round and round the oatmeal chest.[4]

That pictures vividly the calamity of losing the awareness of familiar things and speech dealing with them. Ironically enough, it is a true portrayal of what happened to Yeats himself, when in his later years he cut himself off from what had been a great source of poetic energy, poems enriched with concrete images. He was kidnaped into the cloud land of theosophy and Eastern mysticism, and "lost patience to watch for nearer beauties that once held him, the 'wet strawberry leaves,' 'the mice in the barley sheaves,' 'bubbles in the frozen pool.' " That may happen to a preacher, as well as to a poet. Against it we must watch and pray.

Our struggle to keep free from a technical vocabulary must be like that of Laocoön against the snake which wound itself about him. We all realize, of course, that nuclear physics and philosophical theology cannot be discussed in the vocabulary of Hans Christian Andersen. But the destination of the gospel is not a meeting of a philosophical society. The goal is to speak less like a dictionary and more like a man. I ran across an instance of that not long ago. Here is a dictionary definition of a kiss: "A kiss is the anatomical juxtaposition of two orbicular muscles in a state of contraction." Correct! But perhaps some of you from experience might put it differently.

All this calls for dedicated toil. We are all compelled to say, "With a great price obtained I this freedom to speak clearly." It is not too great a price. There is an impressive report of a visitor to Robert Louis Stevenson in his very last days at Samoa. Stevenson had lost his voice, due to his illness. He could no longer dictate in the usual manner. He wanted so much to finish his novel, *The Weir of Hermiston,* that he had learned the deaf-and-dumb alphabet and the visitor found him dictating with his fingers to his step-daughter, Isobel Strong. We can say of those words, as Emerson said of other words, "They sting, and bite and kick me." If the task of presenting a fictional character was worth that sacrifice, how about the task of presenting the Lord and Master of us all? We get a forcible reminder of the need and power of dedicated workmanship in the history of the Cremona violins. For many years there has been much discussion of the so-called "lost secret of Cremona." Now a historian of music, H. W. Schwartz, tells us that "the supremacy of the work of the great masters of Cremona was not at all due to magic formulae or trade secrets, but to the more prosaic fact of craftsmanship." [5]

Strictly from the standpoint of communication, the great demand can be put in terms of the technique of motion pictures, to give to our message a sight track as well as a sound track. In our presentation, to give something for the eye, as well as for the ear. We know the failure which occurs when in a motion picture the sight track which supplied the picture breaks down and only the voice is left, with the screen blank. We need pictures. John Masefield said, "Chaucer and Keats are my models. They make pictures." In all deep reverence we may say that we have a higher model. He too made pictures.

They are heavenly twins, content and picture, together. And what God hath joined together, let no man in the pulpit put asunder. The supreme demonstration of that, and we mention it in all reverence, is in God's disclosure of Himself. There is, in the epistles of John, the clear statement, "God is Love." There is also the picture, "There they crucified Him." There is the cross, and all the wealth of sacred story gathers about it.

Jesus joined sight and sound, incomparably. Here, for one example, are both. There is the clear, bare statement, "And he told them a parable to the effect that they ought always to pray and not lose heart." Then follows the picture of the truth for the eye and imagination—"In a certain city there was a judge who neither feared God nor regarded man." [6] (Sight track and sound track.) The old story in *The Arabian Nights*, that of Ali Baba and the Forty Thieves, brings to the preacher a touch of longing and envy. Ali Baba found a secret spell in the magic words "Open sesame" which flung open the doors of a treasure cave. If only we could today have some magic words, open sesame, which would swing wide the doors of minds and hearts of those to whom we speak! We do not have that. But we have an approach to it in two words which often are magic, door-swinging words. They are the words "for instance." Those words do open doors of understanding. Thus as we have just seen, the truth that "men ought always to pray." Then, the "open sesame"—"for instance." The doors begin to swing! Again, Jesus saw people who trusted in themselves that they were righteous. And again, "for instance." "Two men went up to the temple to pray." Open sesame! In this, one stern caution must be heeded, always. It follows the pattern of the old proverb, "Never send a boy to do a man's work." Pictures are no substitute for text. Never send merely an illustration or an anecdote to do the work of teaching what can only be done by direct statement and affirmation in plain language.

The inclusive word for this is, of course, imagination, the capacity of forming images. The Gospel, as we have been told, is a gift to the imagination. It bodies forth the forms of things unknown. Information is not enough. One vivid demonstration of imagination at work is in a wonderful treatment in Nathanael J. Burton's Beecher Lectures, *In Pulpit and Parish*. He discusses the graveyard scene in *Hamlet*, where Hamlet picks up a skull. "Alas, poor Yorick, I knew him well." And right before our eyes he clothes a skeleton with life. "A fellow of infinite jest, of most excellent fancy; he hath borne me on his back a thousand times. . . . Here hung those lips I have kissed I know not how oft."

The miracle of creation, of imagination! A pattern of the task of clothing an idea, like the old miracle of Eden, breathing into its nostrils the breath of life. One word with real magic for the preacher is the word "suppose." It vividly carries the truth from one age to another. Dr. John Henry Jowett once put that word down into the midst of the Easter message. His text was, "If Christ be not risen from the dead." All right, he said in effect, "Let's look at it. Suppose everything connected with the Easter faith were removed from the earth." Then he went into detail on what an utterly different word it would be "if Christ be not risen."

Dean Inge, in similar manner, illuminated the idea of the frequent rejection of Jesus and his teaching in our world today by discussing the immigration laws of the United

States. "Suppose," he said, "Jesus were to come to Ellis Island, seeking admission into the United States as an immigrant. For one thing, the quota from Palestine would have been exhausted. Jesus would not have the one hundred dollars demanded from some immigrants. It could easily be proved that he had made many radical statements in his talk. His chances would be slight!"

If we are really to convey and impart truth, we must consider prayerfully attention and interest. For there is very little use to talk to people if they are not paying attention. Some may feel that that is putting the proclamation of the gospel on a low level. It is true that we are not to please men but to please God, to bring men to an encounter with God. Yet all through the Bible there are bugle calls to attention that men may hear, "hear Ye!" "Ho! Everyone that thirsteth," and the sharp word of Jesus, "Listen!"

We have a moral obligation to be interesting. For our gospel is loaded with a life-and-death interest for people. There is a disturbing item in the series of books, published twenty years ago, little volumes on the future of this and that, with a title derived from mythology or history, such as, *Icarus, or the Future of Flying,* and *The Future of Science,* and so forth. When Winnifred Holtby came to write the volume on preaching she gave it the title, *Eutychus, or the Future of Preaching.* Eutychus, you remember, was the man who fell asleep under the preaching of the Apostle Paul. Is the future of preaching to be sleep? There are many who seem to think so.

I feel that a case could be made for the statement that the deadliest enemy of preaching today is not atheism or communism, but sleep. It is quiet but insidious. A yawn is a silent shout, as Chesterton has observed. We might well remember prayerfully the report of the most celebrated tea party ever held, the Mad Hatter's Tea Party in *Alice in Wonderland*. Focus your eyes on the Dormouse. In that party the Dormouse fell asleep six times. He was a tough audience for the talkers. Here is the record: "The Dormouse seemed to be talking in his sleep"; "Wake up, Dormouse, and they pinched it on both sides"; "the Dormouse was going off into a doze"; "the Dormouse fell asleep instantly." Alas, poor Dormouse, I knew him well! He was a member of my congregation. It might be a good thing for the minister to paste up over his study desk a picture of the Dormouse going to sleep. For sleep is an enemy of preaching; most often not snoring sleep, not even nodding sleep, but just staring sleep, where the hearer appears to be giving courteous attention, but in reality, his mind is soaked with laudanum.

I have been fascinated by the names of two little villages in Norfolk, in England, each of which has a parish church. The names are Great Snoring and Little Snoring. I have often felt as though I were the curate of the church at Little Snoring!

A radio announcer said not long ago, "Oh, what a help it would be if we could only hear the click when the program is turned off!" The preacher can see the "click" if he has enough humility to look for it in the faces of his hearers. Humility is a very delicate instrument of help to a preacher in reaching his audience. Then, if he has humility, he can be free to notice what is happening. If a man is not conscious of the wonderful privilege of these people in hearing him, but instead is bowed with awe over the wonder that anyone would listen to him for five minutes, the Lord is with him. Blessed are the poor in spirit, for theirs is the kingdom of the pulpit.

If we are to be fishers of men, we can take a cue from the fishing business. A fisherman who is not casting or using a net needs three things, bait, sinker and cork. So does the fisher of men in his speaking. He needs the lead of solid material, so that his thought does not keep on the surface like a straw. He needs the bait of some interesting material, to attract the hearer. He needs a lively style to keep it afloat.

Three practical cautions are worth, at least, listing. There are two places in a sermon to watch with particular fear and trembling, the beginning and the end, the danger of a delayed start and that of a finish that brings no real conclusion. The danger of the stretched-out introduction is forcibly portrayed in that great book of philosophy, *Mother Goose:*

> On a misty, moisty morning
> And cloudy was the weather
> And there I met an old man
> All dressed in leather.
> I began to smile
> And he began to grin
> And he said, "How do you do?"
> And "How do you do?"
> And "How do you do again?"

There can be too much "How do you do?" To use a figure from building, the sermon may be mostly porch and no house, meriting the verdict, "This man began to build and was not able to finish." A good instance of the immediate dive into a subject is found in one hearer's remem-

brance of an Easter sermon by Joseph Parker in the City
Temple, London, many years ago. This hearer said that Dr.
Parker did not exhaust the first few moments of anticipa-
tion (they were often no more) with which even the dull-
est and most easily predictable of a preacher's opening
words are awaited. He struck in with an idea which was in
fact the germ or substance of everything that followed.

His text was, "I will see you again." Having announced
it, he repeated the words as though he himself were seeing
them for the first time, as it were by a sort of second sight.
"I will see you again." A pause! Then, raising the angle of
his face, and speaking as though the idea had just come to
him, he said *"That is Christianity!"* He proceeded imme-
diately, "If that is not true, then what are all our acts of
worship, what our prayer and monuments and memorials,
what our books, our arguments, our patience? What is anything deep and human, but some makeshift by which we
deceive ourselves, some poor shelter from the intolerable
fact? But, if it be true, "I will see you again," then "Bless
the Lord, O my soul!"

The second point to watch is at the other end. Occasion-
ally it is the simple matter of an overlong farewell, like that
of a caller who seems to have been built into the room and
can't get out. On this matter we may well sit at the feet of
that wise man, Sam Weller. He is reading to his father
a love letter he had written.

"That's a rather sudden pull up, ain't it, Sammy?" in-
quired Mr. Weller. "Not a bit of it," said Sam. "She'll wish
there was more, and that's the great art of letter writing."

It is, and, at times, the art of preaching. The greater

danger, however, is that of the lack of solidity of specification, which will keep the sermon from being in a gaseous
state. Specification of thought and action will furnish direction. The conclusion must deal with a live issue. In a recent
book on big game hunting in Africa the first sentence of
one chapter is, "The first hippo which I ever shot had been
dead a week." There has been too much shooting of dead
hippopotami at the eleven o'clock service on Sundays, issues
from which the real life and pertinence has gone long ago.
A different kind of shooting is needed.

   We should never forget that some of the most notable
sermons in the New Testament were followed by the question, "What shall we *do?*" The preacher has impressed his
hearers with the fact that the message called for some specific action. After the preaching of John the Baptist "the
multitudes asked him 'What then shall we do?' " [7] After
Peter's sermon at Pentecost, "when they heard this they
were cut to the heart and said to Peter and the rest of the
apostles, 'Brethren, what shall we do?' " [8] There is one
verse in the Old Testament in the King James Version of
Ecclesiastes which I hope will not be forgotten. It is a
preacher's text. "Let us hear the conclusion of the whole
matter." [9] There is no substitute for a specific conclusion.
At the end of the sermon, something must be given, something must happen. Otherwise the sermon becomes like the
description of his expensive hotel life, given by a character
of Ring Lardner's. He said, "Everybody puts on their evening clothes like something was going to happen, but it
don't." It is no substitute for that stern necessity to flee
into poetry and announce that

> Lives of great men all remind us
> We can make our lives sublime.

It is a good word which Father Divine invented, "Tangibilizing." It is a good idea—to make a plea tangible.

A third caution here—seizing attention and interest cannot be done by indolence. Very few ministers are in any danger of the common indolence of inactivity. Here and there may be occasional slug-a-bed, who backs into the day at 11:00 A. M. Not often. The real danger is the danger of the indolence of activity. Busy as an ant, precisely so! Busy on a score of employments, until most anything is joyfully greeted as an excuse for escaping the terribly painful exercise of thinking.

One tested way into interest is, of course, narrative. That is true from the day when man first made an intelligible sign. But it may be forgotten that narrative, with the qualities of a good storyteller, selectiveness, imagination and a sense of drama, is a dependable power. Notice the use which St. Paul made again and again of narrative, on occasions of crucial importance. When he was really on trial for his life, besieged by an angry mob at Jerusalem, he puts his case in narrative, interesting dramatic narrative. "As I made my journey and drew near to Damascus, about noon a great light from heaven suddenly shone about me." [10] On trial before Agrippa it is the same narrative on which he depends, "Thus I journeyed to Damascus. . . . At midday, O king, I saw on the way a light from heaven, brighter than the sun, shining round me." [11] The supreme example is Jesus, whose tales have entered the lowliest doors for nineteen centuries.

If we had no other teacher, we could learn the indispen-

sable power of narrative from the agencies of mass communication. If, thinking of the radio and television waves,
we ask the old question, "What are the wild waves saying?"
we get many answers. But amid them, we get one clear
answer. The wild waves much of the time are speaking in
narrative. They are saying, "Once upon a time." "This happened." They are speaking in an old pattern "A certain man
went down from Jerusalem to Jericho." "Two men went up
to the temple to pray."

But this resource, like other things, is something to be
used, and not abused. There have been a good many repor-
torial travel books lately which seem to have been made of a
mass of anecdotes and a dead line. A dead line on Sunday
morning and a mass of anecdotes are not enough.

Over all, permeating all, high above all method, is the
power of a quiet intensity. Not by the might of eloquence,
nor the power of novelty, but by my spirit. The true
preacher rarely has anything new to say about life. He deals
with the experiences of life which were the same essentially
under the pyramids of Egypt as they are under the skyscrapers of New York or Chicago. As E. C. Montague has
said, truly, "The minds of Vergil and Sophocles, Shakespeare and Dante and Goethe seem in the main to have
brooded over just those staple themes which elicit less
memorable expressions of melancholy from Smith, Brown
and Jones." [12] Power in literature and preaching derives
from intensity of reaction to experience, intensity of percep-
tion and emotion. In a real sense the man of power sees and
hears and speaks more intensely.

This does not mean mere exuberance or physical exercise, though often more of even that kind of intensity

would add to the momentum of the word. There is wisdom worth noting in the child's description of a tiger, recorded by A. A. Milne, that "he always seems bigger because of his bounces." There are restrained bounces in speaking which can be used of the Lord. I was impressed several years ago that Eugene Ormandy dislocated a shoulder while leading the Philadelphia Orchestra. I do not know what they were playing. Certainly not Mozart. Perhaps Stravinsky. But at any rate, he was giving all of himself to it! And I have asked myself sadly, "Did I ever dislocate anything, even a necktie?"

But it goes far deeper than that. It is the sharing of intense faith and experience, the expression of actual and immediate experience at firsthand, the vision of the eternal through what is here and now. The result of such intensity is pictured unforgettably in St. Paul's address before Agrippa. We see Agrippa sitting complacently as a judge to hear the argument. Then as Paul goes on, we hear his startled cry of amazement when it dawns on him what Paul is doing—"In a short time you think to make me a Christian!" He is almost stunned. "Why this man is talking to me!" The whole thing has been lifted out of forensics into evangelization. That is the matchless response for which we may work and pray, whether it comes from an Agrippa or a serving maid, "This man is talking to me. He would make me a Christian!"

Now I hope I may say, without too great unfitness, words that I have already recommended. "Hear the conclusion of the whole matter." Recently under my eye there passed an advertisement which called out, "Get the latest in pulpit furniture." I do not know what the latest may be. I said to myself, "Why not get the oldest?" Here are three of the oldest pieces of pulpit furniture tested by the centuries, in the sermon, if preaching is to be a proclamation of God's word.

There must be in the sermon an *altar*. The church must be in the highest sense a meeting house, where the soul meets God—I and thou. That meeting runs all through the Bible, "Thou God seest me." "Against Thee, Thee only have I sinned." "I saw the Lord high and lifted up." "And he said, 'Who art thou, Lord?' And he said, 'I am Jesus, whom you are persecuting.' " "I and thou."

If that is absent, nothing except the trivial is left. Nothing can take the place of the altar. Think of the most common names given to churches which are found in every city in the country. There is *Trinity Church*. What shall anything in church or message profit if there be no presence of the Triune God? How empty a *Church of the Messiah* if there is no gleam of messianic hope! What if in a *Grace Church*, no matter how richly decorated, people are not bowed in awe before the wonder of the grace of God. How empty any *Calvary Church* will be if in its life and pulpit word there is no demonstration of the spirit of Him who on Calvary gave Himself a ransom for many! And in the hundreds of *Christ Churches* over the land, what if it be only a name without the presence of One who came to His disciples, the doors being shut, and stood in their midst. God is the only lasting theme of Christian preaching. Matthew Arnold complained in a supercilious way that life in America was not "interesting." William James snapped right back that the word "interesting" is not a noun, not a substantive; it is an adjective; *nothing* is really interesting in itself, only in relation to somebody or something. Preaching can never be "interesting" for more than an ephemeral moment except in relation to God. God is the substantive, not the adjective.

A mark of this lack, I think, may be found in the frequent evidences of a secular and confused mind, in that many within the church "confuse an aesthetic gratification with worship," or confuse what is called, as though that were the highest tribute that can be paid, "a provocative sermon" with an experience of God, and confuse a good moral resolution for the saving power of God. Without the high altar at the center, we have only a pretty religion which can do no more for us than we can do for ourselves. More than that, any effective compulsion to social service and action stems from the altar of worship. As a theologian has written, "The social gospel in Walter Rauschenbusch and Washington Gladden had its anchorage in an inclusive faith, whose center was God in Jesus Christ, and which in them was mated with a piety which did not ignore the peculiar needs of a man standing in solitariness before the final facts of life." [13]

Again, in our preaching there must be a fireplace, a warmth of love, a glow of heart. That is pictured in two words tied together in a historic experience, and they have been going down the years and centuries tied together—the words "strangely warmed." That is the wonder of the gospel. My heart was strangely warmed! "Did not our hearts burn within us while he talked to us?" Other things will change; that will remain.

> Crowns and thrones may perish
> Kingdoms rise and fall.

The intellectual climate will change, as it is always changing. What seemed the irresistible arguments of other days will lose their relevance and power. This will remain. By the grace of God we can count on this response absolutely and always. Wherever there is a fire on the hearth, men and women will put out their hands to get its warmth.

There must also be a door in our preaching through which people will go out to serve. There has been some discussion of the architecture of the upper room in Jerusalem. Were there any windows in it? Probably not. But from it they could see the world. There was a door opening out. They went out to be witnesses, in Jerusalem, in Judea and Samaria and to the ends of the earth. That must be the result of the presentation of One who said, "I am the door, if any one enters by me, he will go in and out." Some church doors hardly swing at all. Some swing only inward. The doors of a sermon which conveys the word of God in Christ will swing outward, so that over the threshold feet may start out on journeys to need. There is a state law in Connecticut that church doors must swing outward. It is a good law, and a spiritual law as well. There is compulsion as well as reliance in the word given to us. It is our faith and our hope that in our speaking, men and women may be blessed in their coming in and their going out.

VI
Preaching During an Earthquake

ONCE there was a church that "flickered out." That tragic verb does not refer to the sight so familiar to us, and always pathetic, the abandoned church on a rural hillside. It describes a much more distinguished church than that—The First Church of Jerusalem. We can read the beginnings of that epitaph in the book of Acts. The post mortem on that church, like most post mortems, revealed a number of complications. But chiefly, it died of conservatism. It was attached to Jewish rites: it was contented to remain a Jewish sect: it lacked the daring to put new wine into new wineskins. It had no longing to spread the gospel. It is clear from the record in the book of Acts that that church did not want the Apostle Paul to come around. He was a troublemaker, a Christian who went to extremes, and brought disturbance to their serenity.

In his book, *Jesus in the Light of History*, Professor Olmstead writes,

The ten long years of waiting had strained to the utmost their resources; henceforth the mother church was financially poor, and must be supported by the faithful outside of Judea. Although formally recognized as the fountainhead of authority, it had lost all vitality. Firebrands like Stephen, Phillip and Paul stirred up a little trouble, but soon disappeared followed by a sigh of relief, and again the Nazarenes were at peace.[1]

That church left Jerusalem in A. D. 66 and disappeared.

The First Church of Jerusalem was the first demonstration of the inescapable truth, that when a church no longer reaches out, it passes out. The growing tip of the Christian Church was out on the frontier, where it faced the world and its needs. There were brawls, riots, scourgings, danger— in other words, life.

As it was in the beginning, it ever has been. The church which lives is a church on a frontier, geographical, economic and social. That is a basic fact about our present theme, the message and action of the church in economic and social issues. When a church is chiefly concerned with its own preservation and defense, it has ordered its tombstone. A wall of defense always has a subtle way of turning into a tomb. It is when the church emerges from walls, and goes out to a world of need and of change, that it finds life. There is good authority for all this. "He that loseth his life shall find it."

Here we do not bring another program for social action with neat points, from one to ten. We have plenty—and good ones. We have programs enough to serve as road maps from here to heaven. Our concern here is the communication of our message as it enters the realms of living together in all relationships, how we may help the church mediate its gospel by action. It is always difficult when propaganda and demonstration must go together. That has been Russia's problem in East Germany. The demonstration of communism has not matched the propaganda. The church has struggled with the same difficulty. When someone asked Mr. Averill Harriman, the veteran of so many European conferences, how his French was, he said, "My French is excellent, all except the verbs." Quite an exception! It often happens that our Christianity is excellent, "all except the verbs." The nouns are wonderful, "Master, Saviour, Redeemer." The adjectives are inspiring, "noble, divine, sacred." The verbs are often missing. No action. Yet the verb is the sinew of speech. It is the sinew of the gospel, great verbs, "come, go, follow, serve, give, love, share."

There is a beautiful picture of perfect communication by action, which may well serve as a model, in the fourth chapter of Acts. "Now when they saw the boldness of Peter and John . . . they wondered, and they recognized that they had been with Jesus." They saw the deed; they wondered; then they saw the Man behind the deed.

In these realms there is an urgency in conveying the word of God which is hard to exaggerate. Our theme of "Preaching during an Earthquake" follows an old pattern. Our world is having an earthquake. Mountains are being carried into the midst of the sea. There was once some rather effective preaching done during an earthquake. While the building was being shaken down, Paul preached a one-point sermon to the Philippian jailer, "Believe on the Lord Jesus Christ and thou shalt be saved." So our concern is the carrying out through the message and life of the church of some of the implications of Paul's message during an earlier earthquake.

An additional urgency comes from the situation, deeply disturbing, the great gap which exists between ministers and hosts of laymen, a great majority, certainly, in their thinking on social and economic issues. Periodically the chasm widens. It has stretched to an ominous width at the present hour. One distinguished layman, Dr. Douglass S.

Freeman, of Richmond, Virginia, has viewed this division.
He writes of

The grim fact that many laymen have refused to accept or at
least to apply, the economic implications of Christianity in business and government. Some have countenanced one code for
the church and another for the counting house; one code for
the pew and another for the pulpit. They have preached personal unselfishness and upheld national selfishness; they have
given more heed to their brother's church envelope than to his
pay envelope. For fear that they may put the church into
politics, some have failed to have Christianity defend social
justice.[2]

The situation is not too far removed from what happened
to a parade on Fifth Avenue in New York, many years ago,
when the Twenty-seventh Division, returning from World
War I, marched up the avenue. The parade took five hours
to pass. There had to be some interruptions, so that the
crosstown cars could get through. At Twenty-third Street
at one time the parade was suddenly halted, just after the
drum major of a band had passed by, separating the band
from the leader. The drum major went on marching up to
Twenty-ninth Street, swinging his stick gaily up in the air,
while the band was held up six blocks behind.

That lonesome drum major has resemblances to many a
pastor. He is leading on, giving his message in devoted
seriousness, but his band of laymen, who he hoped and
prayed would be following him, are blocked by many obstacles a mile behind, and hardly seem to be moving at all!
If the church is to move in any way like a mighty army, the
gap between the minister and laymen must be shortened.

As a background for the examination of social concern

in the conveying of the Christian message, may we make a few affirmations, swiftly and briefly. Here are four obvious remembrances which must be kept in mind, if the message is not to be fractional and viciously one-sided.

1. As Dr. Henry Sloane Coffin said pointedly years ago, the prophet Amos was not the pastor of the First Presbyterian Church of Bethel. He did not have to come up before the same people and preach forty or fifty times a year. There are tremendous chapters in Amos, but could any church live on them as an exclusive diet served up fifty-two times a year? There is a fallacy in the phrase "a prophetic ministry" as frequently conceived and praised. For what is called a prophetic ministry may be largely a menu of denunciation, and that may be greatly lacking in spiritual vitamins. It is possible for a preacher to follow the program of Lady Britomart in Shaw's *Major Barbara*, who was "the incarnation of morality" and "whose conscience is clear and whose duty done when she has called everybody names." John Morley, when editing a daily paper in the middle of the nineteenth century, once asked a young journalist what his specialty was. He replied, "Invective." A poor specialty for a preacher! The spiritual content of straight denunciation is rather low. It is easy to push this too far, but it does come into the picture.

2. A church cannot live on a series of alarm and excursions. There are great evils to be attacked. God pity us if we ever forget them! But there can easily be a false simplification of the task of the preacher as leading a series of attacks. Consider the case of Paul Revere, the beloved hero on a galloping steed, striking out sparks in the night,

Ready to ride and spread the alarm
To every Middlesex village and farm.

Suppose that on Monday night he rode through, crying, "The British are coming!" Then, on Tuesday night he would come again, at the same time with the same shout, "The British are coming!" Then on Wednesday night, "The Swedes are coming!" and on Thursday, "The Russians are coming!" By Saturday night the farmers and townsmen would bang the windows shut and tell him to go home and go to bed. That is the weakness of a Paul Revere in the pulpit.

More than that, such a series of alarms does not face the question of motivation. Merely to announce what are the things that need to be done does not face the prior question of getting people to want to do them. One of the saddest sights I ever saw was rows of irrigation ditches in Montana in the midst of a drought. There were plenty of places for water to run if there were any water. So, in churches, there is little use to announce the plenty of things for people to do if they do not want to do them. We get the problem of motivation in Paul's great appeal, "I beseech you, brethren, by the mercies of God." There must be imparted the sense of the mercies of God, which brings the power of compulsion into life.

3. There is a deceptive stimulation in a minister's merely getting "something off his chest." When a person is doing that, he is never preaching. There is an intoxication about the vigor and denunciation, something like that which comes from a good slug of whiskey. Our problem is to bring the conviction of collective guilt, such as was expressed by William Morris, when he said, "I never see a man drunken,

brutal, without shame, without feeling that I had a hand in it."

4. Remember also that sometimes preaching on social and economic issues may be an unrecognized escape from the harder task of bringing about a change in the inner life. This matter of escape for the preacher runs both ways. He may escape from the social responsibility of the pulpit into an easy piety which will be a soothing lullaby to a well-fed, complacent congregation. God save us from that! But we can also escape from the responsibility of building up spiritual stability in people, through the luxury of some kind of a heated onslaught.

There is a very real, though unintended pattern for carrying the meaning of the Christian revelation into disputed areas of life in the record of Jesus' sending out seventy disciples. We read, "The Lord appointed seventy others, and sent them on ahead of him, two by two, into every town and place where he himself was about to come." [3] "Where he himself is about to come"—that is both our commission and our reliance. We are to go into the areas of thought and action where Christ is about to come, the no-man's lands not yet brought under his dominion, and into which his light was barely penetrated. Christ has not yet come into many of the gladiatorial contests of money-making, not yet come into the dark jungle of race relations, or into the red fields of war. We are to be his messengers, going into those unreached lands where he is about to come.

Our commission is to go into unoccupied territory, across dangerous frontiers. There has been far too much loitering around the Home Base, a safe distance from the line of battle. One of our greatest weaknesses is that so many have given up seeking. The only command they hear is, "As you were." They have established a base, but they do not push out from it to explore the territory that lies beyond. There have been too few probing thrusts. Their one song is, "We're Tenting Tonight on the Old Camp Ground." Some of the greatest hours of Christian history have been when disciples have gone out ahead, where Jesus was about to come. In the eighteenth century Wilberforce and Clarkson went out two by two into the blighted land of human slavery where Jesus was about to come. And he came. Later Washington Gladden and Walter Rauschenbusch went out two by two into the strongly defended fortress of economic life into which Jesus was about to come.

One truth has been more than amply demonstrated. Unless there is clear and emphatic teaching on social questions, a church develops pernicious anemia. Its lifeblood deteriorates, unable to sustain combat strength for "God's Holy War." If all we can hear in church is the pale and pious echo of the voice of society around us, the gospel is not imparted. A church can become a cave of the echoes. That was true of a large part of the church in Germany before Hitler, other than the Confessional Church which made such a heroic witness, and having done all, stood. A large part of the church was unfitted to cope with the growing Nazi power, because so many had withdrawn from the life about them and were concerned only with questions of doctrine, piety and polity.

"If the trumpet give forth an uncertain sound," not very much will happen. Canon Alexander of St. Paul's Cathedral in London has estimated, by what kind of measurements I do not know, that the Cathedral is moving down Fleet

Street at the rate of one inch every hundred years. There are many who are convinced that the church must move faster than that!

There is one other remembrance to keep visible in this whole field of economic and political questions. It is a rather gloomy one. It is that some people will never change their opinions in these realms. That statement does not spring from cynicism, but from realism. To realize that in advance is to be armored against being overwhelmed when we meet it. The attachments to accustomed practices and ideas go too deep in the mind to be affected by any evidence. They may sing the 57th Psalm, "My heart is fixed, O God." But it really means "my mind is fixed—rigid, petrified. It is what the psychologist calls "area rigidity." That is, being open-minded on many things, but in this particular area of interest, never. There is only one thing harder than to get a new idea into such a rigid mind, and that is to get an old one out of it. There is not much more chance for a new idea to get into the mind than for a breeze to blow through a billiard ball. In both, there is the same kind of material. Thus we have a modern version of the old story of Bluebeard, the locked room where no one must enter. It is not that this forbidden room conceals shameful crimes. Not at all. It is just that this room must never be opened. We can remember that there were people whom Jesus did not win, whose minds he could not change. About them he pronounced some of the most terrible words he ever spoke, "Let them alone." There is no use! St. Paul met this rigidity of mind and dealt with it realistically. He said, "Lo, we turn to the Gentiles." Jesus, who said of some of the scribes and Pharisees, "Let them alone," also said, "Let the little children come unto me." That gives us a new field of effort, Christian nurture and education which can shape minds open to the mind of Christ, wherever it may lead. This remembrance does not absolve us from a lifetime of patient teaching and persuasion. It does fortify us against undue optimism.

We can, at least, do some spying in the enemies' territory by looking at five of the obstacles to the communication of our Christian faith as it relates to the making of a brotherly community among men:

1. The first is an obstacle in ourselves, in the church. We have not done enough clear teaching on the social relevance of our gospel. We have not transmitted that. By failing there, the pulpit has turned over the minds of many laymen to the most vicious forces now operating in America. By its silence in this area the pulpit has often said to the demagogues, to the John T. Flynns and the Westbrook Peglers, and to a host of other minor and major apostles of confusion, "I am not planning to do anything with the minds of these people. You take over." And, make no mistake about it, they do. One reason there have been such great inroads of fear and jittery hysteria among laymen of all the Protestant churches on the subject of Christian social action, is that congregations have not received enough sharp and sustained teaching in the realm of the application of Christian faith to social and economic issues. If the pulpit gives no teaching, the demagogues do, incessantly. So we have had in the last four years the astounding spectacle of hosts of sincere laymen taking the interpretation of what the Protestant churches stand for, from an ill-informed Catholic like John T. Flynn, whose real ignorance of Protestantism gives

you a rough idea of infinity. We have an obligation to save our people from being made gullible by unchristian forces. If they are sent out as sheep among wolves, they can at least be taught what the wolf looks like so that they do not mistake it for a fawn! We may well take a leaf from the book of Abraham Lincoln, who wrote to General Mc-Clellan, "If you are not planning to do anything with the army, will you lend it to me for a while?" So, in all deep reverence we may think of Christ saying to his minister, "If you are not planning to do anything with the people of this church, will you lend them to me for a while?"

2. A second great obstacle to the transmission of Christian evaluations in these fields is *nostalgia*. Now, the living remembrance of past days has been for all of us a beautiful thing. Without it, life would be reduced to the bleakness of the one dimension, the present. We all sigh, on occasion, and ought to, "I remember, I remember." And, "Backward, O backward, turn time in your flight." But when a sentimental longing for the past becomes the whole climate of mind, it is a deadly disease. Churches have died from it. It has been an unrivaled block to ethical action. It becomes the canonization of the simplicities, usually mythical, of the good old days, of ideas and actions, inadequate to present complexities. It becomes a sort of Currier and Ives religion, an Old Oaken Bucket religion, and as such, a deadly rival of Christianity. Such measuring of everything by the backward look through the haze steels minds against any religious and ethical advance. They cannot hear the liberating words, "You have heard it said. . . . But I say unto you."

3. A third obstacle is the habit of living by slogans. By

dint of loud repetition unexamined affirmations come to be the supreme creed to multitudes, the final word of authority, all the way from shaving soap to the United Nations. Bernard Shaw wrote that "the world is largely governed by considerations that occur to stockbrokers in the first five minutes." That is an exaggeration, but it is borne out in those who live by unscrutinized slogans. William Morris said he wanted to take the "mumbo jumbo" out of the world. That is our calling, brethren. The voice of mumbo jumbo, as it shouts in economic and social propaganda, is powerful. It gives a frightening echo of Vachel Lindsay's "Mumbo Jumbo, God of the Congo, Mumbo Jumbo will hoodoo you" if you are not "regular." We can challenge slogans with puncturing questions. Here is the man—and his name is legion—whose stock dismissal of the vast issue of medical care in the United States is to mutter the slogan "Socialized Medicine." We can ask, "What do you make of the fact that of the first two million men drafted in World War II, 52 per cent were rejected? Is that the best we can do?" Jesus went about challenging many of the axioms of his time.

4. A fourth obstacle is sometimes respectability. Possible ideas and actions are weighed on one scale, "Is it what the respectable classes do?" Jesus met it. "Why does your master dine with sinners?" All through the gospels we can hear the grumble of critics like the distant roar of the sea. His concern for the last, the least and the lost was out of the bounds of respectability. There is a lovely word of Mr. Chesterton's mother quoted in his autobiography. His father had prospered so much and won the esteem of the community so greatly, that he was elected a vestryman of

the church. His mother protested against his accepting the honor. "Oh, Edward," she exclaimed passionately, "we'll be so respectable. We've never been respectable. Let's not begin now!" We can adapt that fear and say, The Church in its greatest hours has never been respectable. It has consorted with sinners. It has reached out its hands to the rag, tag and bobtail of humanity.

5. Finally, one obstacle to the transmission of teaching in the realm of business and social issues is one which covers a multitude of sins. It is the practice of absolutizing the merely relative. Ways of life are hallowed by habit, beloved myths are lifted up and given an absolute value. The myth may be "the American way of life," "free enterprise" or a political party, or the nation. It has surrounded itself with an emotional aura which hedges it about with divinity. It becomes undebatable.

Nostalgia prevents a very important, indeed, an indispensable intellectual operation, stripping the *status quo* of moral sanctity. Herbert Spencer gave the perfect example of this vicious-making the relative absolute in his classic declaration that "modern business enterprise represented the highest good—the rational outcome of the universe, the ideal toward which the whole course of nature ever tends." A disturbing symbol of this tendency is the fashion of building banks in the form of temples. To many people, they are holy temples.

In the antireligious museum in Moscow, housed in what was once a great church, there is an icon on which a portrait of Czar Nicholas II was painted over the face of Christ. That is a picture of what happens when the relative is made absolute. If the Soviets used icons, the face would be different, Stalin instead of Nicholas. A typical American icon would have a flag or dollar sign painted over the face of Christ. This process is the most popular form of rejection of the old command, "Thou shalt have no other gods before me"!

The toughness and durability of these obstacles make clear the inadequacy of many familiar ways of presenting the social relevance of the gospel, or rather, ways of avoiding them. One way not good enough is that found by the Lynds in their book *Middletown*. That is, the resonant reiteration of what Middletown already knows and believes. No one was ever stoned for that. It is no accident that with such a ministry the high day of the church year is Mother's Day. Middletown believes in mothers. The symbol of that type of religion becomes not a cross, but a carnation.

So it is possible to become magnificently emotional in a social vacuum. That has gone, all too often, with an absence of any initiative in attack. In the special Revised Version of the New Testament used by such people, the text is missing, "We contend against the world rulers of this present darkness." Sometimes, when confronted by the marauding powers of evil, the preacher and the church merit the words with which Robert Burns addressed a mouse:

> Wee sleekit, cowrin', tim'roous beastie
> Oh, what a panic's in thy breastie!
> Thou need na start away sae hastie
> Wi' bickering brattle!

In the book of Revelation we have stirring pictures of a fellowship of Christians at bay, fighting a beast. But in these latter days, instead of fighting the predatory beast of evil, quite a number of people give it a gentle pat on the head and say, "Nice pussy." Such a ministry is "comfortable," but in the degenerate modern sense of the words, not the stout original sense. When William Bradford wrote of his minister, John Robinson, that he was "a comfortable minister," he did not have in mind upholstered relaxation. John Robinson did not believe in salvation by siesta. He brought comfort in the sense of fortification for endurance and effort.

Our chief concern, however, is always the positive rather than the negative. What are the helps to communication in this realm? What resources do we have for genuine meditation?

One help is obvious, but often disregarded. That is to find the source of our message in our gospel. Then the sermon does not come as a strange and questionable addition to the word of God. One elementary handicap that often hinders preaching on social issues is that it is separated from the preaching of the gospel. Frequently a congregation does not respond to presentation of social implications of the faith, not because the people are born reactionaries, which they are not, but because the man is not preaching. They look up bewildered and say, "Jesus, I know, and Paul I know. But who are you?"

The preacher's concern must always be not change for the sake of any social change but to help people find what might be the will of God as a guidance for action. That is one reason for the effectiveness of Biblical preaching, for in that we are dealing with things which are so largely accepted by the congregation.

One recent instance of this was reported to me recently.

A pastor had been urging support for a low-cost housing project in the community. An irate hearer snarled at him, "Why don't you just preach the gospel? That is what we pay you for. Jesus never talked about low-cost housing projects." The pastor replied, "Oh, brother, if you only read the gospels once in a while you might know something. You might know that Jesus gave his sternest denunciation to the real-estate lobby of Jerusalem, men who devoured widows' houses, and made low-cost housing impossible for poor widows."

All this requires a high faith in two respects. One is the faith that God's word in Christ does throw a light on our path, wherever we may go. That does not mean that we find in the Bible any detailed program to follow in complex circumstances. We do not. We do find basic principles which will guide the most honest thinking we can bring. It was said in tribute to Coleridge that wherever you go in literary criticism, you always find Coleridge coming back. It is our faith that wherever you go in our baffling social world, you find Jesus coming back. The entrance of his word gives light to minds dedicated to finding what seem to be expressions of his truth.

The other faith is that in the effort to find ways of bringing love into all our relationships, we are not off on a whim of our own, but that God is our reliance. One of the most impressive cartoons ever published was that by Will Dysart in London during the lowest spot of the depression in the 1930's. It showed daring in the drawing of a figure representing God, with Jesus standing by his side. Underneath were printed the words, "We are powerless, my son. The banks have spoken." That represents crudely but truly a real faith, that God is not powerless *after* the banks have spoken. The last word on Calvary was not spoken by iron nails. The last word in our shared life is not spoken by banks.

One dedication must be made—to handle the word of God with reverence; not to import into it what is not there. All of us are doomed to fail partially in this. The word is refracted through our own individual minds. But we can agonize to do it, until we die. Unless we are willing to put this stern discipline on ourselves we have no right to speak. Charles Lamb, looking at Robert Haydon's massive spread of canvas on which he painted the "Triumphal Entry into Jerusalem," made a comment to remember. He said, "The face of Jesus looks remarkably like Haydon." To that we can all say fervently, "Let us pray." We are all in danger of making our portrait of Christ look suspiciously like ourselves. We can be saved only by grace—and honest exegesis.

There is a great phrase in the 27th Psalm which underlies the whole teaching function of the church, "to inquire in his temple." That is what we should do in the temple, not only "behold the beauty of the Lord" but use the mind —inquire. There used to be a room in churches, in connection with evangelistic services, called "the inquiry room." The whole sanctuary should be an inquiry room. But to "inquire"—to bring the mind to the task of thinking through the meanings of faith, is the last thing many people do in the temple. They sing, they speak, they shout, they give, sometimes they quarrel, often they eat. A pastor recently described his new flock as "the eatingest church you ever saw." We need the grace of inquiring, and the preacher in his spirit and words must cultivate that grace.

A help is found in the continuous stress on one great principle which covers much ground, to measure the world as Jesus measured it. He measured it in terms of people. That principle is like the magic tent in the Oriental fairy story, made of material so delicate that it could be folded up and held in the palm of a man's hand; yet when it was unrolled and set up it could shelter an army of thousands of men. So the principle of the worth of a person in the sight of God, as revealed in Christ, guides in person-to-person relationship and spreads out to include a world. This truth is compressed in an antithesis of Barth's, "We believe in a civilization of things; Christ believed in a civilization of persons."

Preaching must bring first aid to the imagination, so that men may see the world as Jesus saw it. A poet has fancied the wonder of the sharpening of our senses,

> To see
> With the eye
> of the fly
> . . . .
> Or with the furred ear
> Of the deer
> To hear what no others can hear.[4]

That would be an exquisite heightening of the senses. We couldn't endure it. But we can have something better. We can hope to see with the eyes of Christ that what was great to him may be great to us, and what was small to him may be small to us. Think of the contrast between the eyes of Jesus and those of his disciples. When they came up to Jerusalem, they saw buildings. They cried, "Look, Teacher, what wonderful stones and what wonderful buildings!" [5]

Jesus also said "Look!" But he saw people. He said, "Look at that woman over there, putting in two copper coins into the treasury. Out of her poverty she has put in everything she had." He saw the people who were deprived of the privilege of using the Temple as a house of prayer. He saw defrauded widows. If we can help people to look at the world as Jesus did, we give them a new slide rule by which to measure. Then they can see that many of the world's boasted advances become its diseases, measured by the effect on people. They can see that while our society has done wonders with the mechanical arts of multiplication, it has done far less with the ethical art of division. They will be more able and ready to go on to the dangerous edge of things for the sake of people, for whom Christ died. As a footnote to that, I would add this word of exhortation, not to allow ourselves to be browbeaten by any theological bully who hurls at us the word "activism." It is usually spoken with a curl of scorn on the lip. Of course we all understand that no acts or number of acts can be a substitute for an encounter with God. That was the mistake of the rich young ruler, when he asked, "What good thing must I *do* to inherit eternal life?" The answer was, no good thing. Eternal life cannot be inherited by doing any good thing or any number of them. Yet that word "activism" can be made to minimize too much of the Christian experience and life. After all we worship a God who acts. St. Paul was tainted with activism—in the rescue of a girl from her exploiters, we have a model of all efforts to rescue girls from exploitation; in the clash with the worshipers of Diana in Ephesus, we have a model for a clash with all that is put in the place of God. Surely we will not forget that the story of the launching of Christ's church in the world is called the book of Acts!

One constant aim will be to strive to develop in people a sensitiveness to evil, some share in the sensitiveness of mind which Jesus manifested. He had a nervous alertness to the presence of faith and goodness; equally quick to detect the contamination of the air which came from dark purposes and designs. "See their thoughts." "He knew what was in man."

This quality of spirit, so greatly needed, found expression in the strong words of Peter Cartwright, the frontier evangelist. Coming into a little settlement which was a sinkhole of iniquity he loudly announced, "I smell hell." He had not yet seen the evil, nor heard it. He smelled it. He had the nose of a fox hound for wrong. It is a great gift. A sharp nose is an instrument for ethical evaluation. If we do not have it, we become like the idols denounced in the 115th Psalm, "Noses have they, but they smell not." In the heyday of *laissez-faire* economics, when the doctrine of no government interference put its blessing on the slaughter of child workers, there were a few Christians who made violent protests. They did not have any equipment of scholarly economic theory. They had something better— noses. They smelled the hell covered with fair words. There are processes and customs today in industry, race relations and politics which literally "smell to heaven." We need the training and consecration of the nose.

Perhaps we need another verse to that noble hymn ascribed to St. Andrew of Crete, based on the Greek of the seventh century,

Christian dost thou see them
On the holy ground . . .

The verses ask the questions, "Dost thou see them?" "Dost thou feel them?" and "Dost thou hear them?" We need another verse, "Christian dost thou smell them?"

Again, if we are to impart the message, we need the courage of the specific. The individualistic commitment to abstract virtues is not enough to make any devils tremble or to assault any stronghold of wrong. The courage of the specific does not mean the indulgence of an insufferable dogmatism about actions. It does not mean the identification of Christianity with any order or institution or proposal. We cannot say that Christian teaching demands that any needed reform, such as the elimination of racial discrimination, demands federal rather than state action. But we can get the subject raised in specific terms so that our preaching shall not be a pea-soup fog. Speaking in specific words will get us into trouble. But there is no other way to avoid the vicious sentimentalism of the advocacy of ends without the provision of means, or the sentimentalism of refusing to carry an idea to its logical conclusion. I do not know any picture of the futility of ends without means than a bit of history of Oxford University. After years of debate the dons of one college finally voted to allow the buildings to be lighted with gas. But when asked to grant permission for gas pipes to be installed, they stoutly refused. They were in favor of gas in general but not gas in pipes.

Jesus did general teaching such as the Beatitudes, and the persuasion to trust God. He also had the courage of the specific, as in his rejection of the whole ceremonial code. Jesus was not crucified for saying, "Consider the lilies, how they grow." What brought him to the cross, as far as men were concerned, was saying, "Consider the thieves in the temple, how they steal."

It is the specific action which puts our faith squarely against the ruling anti-Christian and sub-Christian codes of our time. Recall the shout which greeted the Christian martyrs in the Colosseum, "To the lions with the atheists!" Strange-sounding words, to call the Christians "atheists." But the crowd was right. They were atheists. They did not believe in the gods of Rome, in Venus, in Bacchus, in a philandering Jupiter or the emperor. We need the cultivation of a stubborn atheism, of Christians making clear that they do not believe in the gods of our market places. Saying, "we do not believe in Bacchus, or in Venus the goddess of lust, or in Mercury the fleet-footed God of clever thievery, or in Mars or Vulcan." Vulcan is the chief god of many Americans at the present hour, the god of the forge, the armorer. His altars are everywhere; our whole economy depends on him. His sign in which we trust is a pillar of smoke from giant chimneys by day and a pillar of fire by night.

If we are to worship the God and Father of our Lord Jesus Christ we must be more aggressive atheists about all others. For all these needs there are resources in passages of Scripture, which seem to have been made for that situation or need from the foundation of the world. Take the basic need, to get people to change their minds. What a story there is at the crucifixion, about a man big enough to change his mind on the basis of new evidence, the centurion who said when he had watched it all, "Surely, this was a son of God." Take another attitude we are trying to in-

culcate—of seeing the effect of present conditions on
people. Bring the familiar picture of Jesus looking at his
proud city, Jerusalem, with clear vision, with love, with
painful grief. Do we ever see our city as Jesus saw Jerusalem,
or do we hang an iron curtain at the end of our pleasant
street? Or take that text about war and the things that lead
to war. Out of its context, of course, but as a picture it has
complete validity—the words of Martha to Jesus at the
grave of Lazarus, "Lord, if you had been here, my brother
would not have died." What a text for war, "Lord, if you
had been here, in 1914, 1939, nineteen fifty what? if Christ
had been in our minds and life, our brothers would not
have died. "Or what we have just been speaking of—a plea
for a Christian skepticism. Take the text, "Lord, increase
our faith." We must all pray that. But we must also pray,
"Lord, increase our doubt." When we hear the solemn
assertion that the way to secure peace is to arm so strongly
that all nations will be scared to death of us, Lord, increase
our doubt. When we are told, as we often are, that there
is nothing the matter with the world that more science and
intelligence cannot cure, Lord, increase our doubt. Or take
that truly terrible text, "He that believeth not shall be
damned," in the addition which has been made to the un-
finished gospel of Mark. We do not accept it in the connection in which it appears. But how tragically true of our
world! If we do not believe in the way of life that Jesus
taught and lived, we shall be destroyed. Right now our
world is poised on the dizzy edge of disaster through in-
stitutionalized skepticism about the teaching of Jesus. Or
consider what we must stress without rest, the final motive
power for action. "Love one another, even as I have loved

you." Those three words "even as I" are high-tension wires carrying immeasurable power. "Love so amazing, so divine" demands!

One other help is to remember that we are <u>advocates for unseen clients.</u> The people whose cause we plead are rarely ever in the pews in front of us. It is difficult to speak for those who are not present to those who are present. The conventional preacher can easily forget those out of the range of vision. To remember them calls for a costly offer-ing—a dedicated imagination. The preacher must do his work surrounded by a great cloud of witnesses of two sorts, those who have gone before, and a cloud of clients. The clients are pictured in the vivid words of George Adam Smith who said that the Prophet Amos could always see "the pinched faces of starved peasants looking through the picket fences." No fence must shut them out. They are the people in need, far away, across the tracks, across the sea. But, much farther away, across the lines of likeness, of color, of class, of religion. If their cause is to plead at all in the hearing of many in the congregation, it will be pleaded by us.

In the realm of labor this means that we contend for the rights and needs of workers beyond those of a well-cared-for machine. Though even on that level machines have often been better cared for than men. Machines were more valu-able. Beyond that is the need for the fundamental dignity of a human being, the need for freedom of action, self-ex-pression. We have in industry come a long way from the early days of Virginia, when a minister in the colony asked for help in founding a school. He told the attorney general of England that the colonists had "souls to save." The attorney general made a historic reply, "Damn your souls, make tobacco!" Yet we do not have to go back to 1620 to find those words used as the watchword in industry. Many can remember the tragic Pullman strike, when the stand of the company was not more than two inches away from "Damn your souls, make Pullman cars!" One thing deserves remembrance. Two things, really. One is that we are as Christians opposed to the use of hard power just because any group has it, whether unions or employees or any other group, just as we are against it when communist Russia makes an irresponsible use of sheer power. But we must remember that in a labor dispute, in a strike, labor is the most highly visible of the two contending forces. We can all see a striker; we can see a picket marching up and down, we can see a mill or a mine shut down. We cannot see the books of the company. They are hidden away in a vault. It is very easy to get mad at strikers who threaten our gasoline or coal supply. It is not so easy to get mad at a company's ledger which we cannot see. And yet, giving way to blind emotion, or to self-interest, without the evidence of the ledger, we are liable to get an entirely distorted idea of the situation.

In the realm of race relations one immediate thing for us all is to raise one prayer, morning and night, that we may never grow used to the pagan denials of brotherhood in Christ which are found in codes of conduct regarding race, in discrimination, segregation and exploitation. We must pray that we may retain the capacity of being deeply hurt by the hurt of our brothers. For as Barth has written, "If there is no great agony in our heart, there will be no great

words on our lips." We must feel the horror and terror that
the Ancient Mariner felt!

> The very deep did rot, Ah, Christ,
> That this should ever be.
> Yea, slimy things did crawl with legs
> Upon a slimy sea.

All over America in the treatment of racial groups, slimy
things do crawl on a slimy sea. We can work to keep in high
visibility the practical effects of racial injustice, its weak-
ening of the whole life of the country, and its vitiating our
influence on the world. In particular, on one level, we can
keep reiterating the tremendous economic and financial
costs of segregation. Beyond that we can make clear the
spiritual disaster which comes with a tolerance of unchristian race relations. The effect has already been mentioned
that no doctrine can live in the intellect that does not
renew itself in experience. If the doctrine of the love of God
does not renew itself in the practice of love to all of God's
children, it will become merely an academic affair.

Finally in the realm of international relations, we will
not settle that in a few minutes or hours. We can only here
bring up some truths to be stressed, in season and out of
season.

One text for all "out-of-season" thinking is, "The Lord
direct your hearts into the patience of Christ." The hardest
virtue to practice in these days, in situations where there
seems to be no exit, is patience. It is so much harder than
any kind of blind fury and action. But it ranks high among
the adequate virtues. It is needed against a rising flood of
"Get it over, somehow." It is that word "somehow" that's
the rub!

Constant also is the obvious truth that in the world grown smaller through technology, the individual's geographical responsibility has grown larger. When H. V. Kaltenborn was managing editor of the *Brooklyn Eagle*, he kept on his desk a sign which read, "Always remember that a dog fight in Brooklyn is more important than a revolution in China." Too many people have accepted that devil's lie. Now we are learning that a revolution in China results in funerals in Brooklyn, and funerals are more important than dog fights. "The man about town must become the man about planet."

Yet when we speak of Christian guidance in the international realm, there are many who say, "There goes the preacher again, taking off into the wild blue yonder, bringing the beautiful sentimentalism of Jesus into the hard brutal realm of foreign policy." There is a short answer to that in three words, "Is that so?" Take that "romantic optimism" of Jesus about human brotherhood and then look at the world. What is under the convulsion in Asia, deeper than the hunger for food and the hunger for land? We are watching the bursting of a century's pent-up resentment of the treatment by the white man of the colored races as inferior. They are tired of the denial of brotherhood and are not having any more of it, thank you. Here is Premier Nehru speaking,

The West has too often despised the Asian and African and still in many places denies not only equality of right but even common humanity and kindliness.

Here is Justice Douglas of the Supreme Court,

I have recently left the villages of Asia with fear in my heart, fear for the safety and durability of the civilization of the West. We of the West have gone to these other continents harshly, arrogantly, and oppressively. Our attitudes have been haughty and overbearing. From the earliest days our emissaries have been freebooters and buccaneers of one kind and another. . . .⁶

We did not have the mind of Christ—we despised that mind, and we have what we have. So far from being sentimentalism, Jesus brought the hardest piece of economic and political realism that has ever been injected into the world's thinking.

Again we can strive to free people from the illusion that there will be a god from the machine to end our time and troubles. That is what happened often in Greek drama; when things got desperate, a god appeared in a machine. The answer to that illusion is found in a headline, repeated many times in the last two years, "GLOBEMASTER CRASHED." It is a delusive name for an airplane, "Globemaster." No machine can be a "globemaster." Only the Master can be that. Nations, our own included, have believed too long in the gospel according to *Pinafore* instead of in the Gospel. You know the Pinafore gospel, as proclaimed by the British tar:

His energetic fist should be ready to resist a dictatorial word.
His nose should pant and his lips should curl;
His cheeks should flame and his brow should furl;
His bosom should heave and his heart should glow
And his fist be ever ready with a knock down blow.

We must deal with causes rather than the symptoms which result from deeper causes.

In his description of a bomb test in Nevada in the spring of 1952, David Lawrence used a phrase which is an inclusive one in a far deeper sense than the one in which he used it. Describing the tension of the last few seconds before the bomb was dropped he wrote, "Then there was a light out of this world, with the intensity of a hundred suns." A great phrase! In the bombs bursting in air we do get a "light out of this world." Our only hope comes from out of this world—a light not with the intensity of a hundred suns, but with the infinitely greater intensity of God. "God is light," and in his light we have light for reliance and direction for action, "The light of the glory of God in the face of Jesus Christ."

Notes

I. A Babel of Tongues

1. J. B. Priestly, *Delight*. Harper & Brothers, 1949, p. 45.
2. *The New Yorker*. Copyright, 1939, by The New Yorker Magazine, Inc., and used by permission.
3. George M. Trevelyan, *Biography and Other Essays*. Longmans, Green & Co., 1949.
4. Olin Downes in *The New York Times*.
5. John 7:15.
6. Acts 4:13.
7. William Butler Yeats, *Collected Poems, 1951*. Copyright, 1951, by The Macmillan Company, and used by permission.
8. Rupert Hart-Davis, *Hugh Walpole*. The Macmillan Company, 1952.
9. Jer. 9:23.
10. F. W. H. Myers, *St. Paul*. Used by permission of Macmillan and Co., London.
11. Mark 10:42–43.
12. Arthur Guiterman, *Gaily the Troubadour*. Copyright, 1936, by E. P. Dutton and Co., and used by permission.

II. The Faith Once Delivered—Yesterday and Today

1. *Bolts of Melody, New Poems of Emily Dickinson*, edited by Mabel Loomis Todd and Millicent Todd Bingham. Copyright, 1945, by Millicent Todd Bingham, and used by permission of Harper & Brothers.

2. Heinrich Heine, *Works of Prose*, edited by Hermann Kesten, translated by E. B. Ashton. L. B. Fischer, 1943.
3. H. G. Wells, *Mind at the End of Its Tether*. William Heinemann, Ltd., 1945.
4. T. S. Eliot, *The Idea of a Christian Society*. Harcourt, Brace and Company, Inc., 1940.
5. Siegfried Sassoon, *Collected Poems*. Copyright, 1949, by The Viking Press, and used by permission.
6. "Christina."
7. *Pilgrim's Progress*.
8. *The Doctrine of the Word of God*. (Prof. G. T. Thompson's translation of the first half-volume of the *Kirklische Dogmatick*), p. 188.
9. *Union Seminary Review*, June, 1951.
10. Ps. 8:3, 4, 9.
11. Luke 5:26.
12. Acts 3:10.
13. Holy Ghost Sonnet.
14. Acts 2:13.
15. Acts 17:6.
16. *The Complete Poems of Emily Dickinson*. Little, Brown and Company, 1927.
17. Isa. 6:1.
18. II Tim. 1:12.
19. Rev. 3:20.
20. Luke 11:5–6.

III. To Serve the Present Age

1. Matt. 9:36.
2. T. S. Eliot, *Collected Poems*. Copyright, 1937, by Harcourt, Brace and Company, Inc., and used by permission.
3. A. E. Housman, *Last Poems*. Copyright, 1922, by Henry Holt & Co., Inc., and used by permission.
4. Stephen Spender, *The Still Center*. Faber and Faber, 1939, and used by permission.

5. David Seabury, *Adventures in Self-discovery.* Whittlesey House, 1938.
6. Phil. 4:11–12.
7. Act V, sc. 3.
8. Eunice Tietjens, *Profiles from China.* Copyright, 1919, by Alfred A. Knopf, Inc., and used by permission.
9. Lloyd Lewis, *Sherman, Fighting Prophet.* Harcourt, Brace and Company, Inc., 1936.
10. Peter Viereck, *Tenor and Decorum, Poems, 1940–1948.* Copyright, 1948, by Charles Scribner's Sons, and used by permission.
11. Ps. 71:1 (A.V.)
12. II Cor. 4:8.
13. Eph. 3:18.
14. *The Church.* Report of a theological Commission on Faith and Order. Student Christian Movement Press, 1951.
15. II Pet. 3:11–12.

IV. He Opened the Book

1. Gordon Poteat, *We Preach Not Ourselves.* Harper & Brothers, 1914, pp. 4–5, 6.
2. Charlotte Perkins Gilman.
3. Osbert Sitwell, *Laughter in the Next Room.* Longmans, Green and Co., 1949.
4. George M. Trevelyan, *Autobiography and Other Essays.* Little, Brown & Co., 1948.
5. I Cor. 13:9.
6. Dorothy Sayers, *Creed or Chaos.* Methuen & Co., Ltd., 1947.
7. Francis Thompson, "O World Invisible We See Thee." Burns, Oates & Washbourne, Ltd. Used by permission of the publisher and Mr. Wilfred Meynell, executor.
8. C. J. Furnas, *Voyage to Windward.* William Sloane Associates, 1951.

9. Emil Ludwig, *Napoleon*, translated by Eden and Cedar Paul. Garden City Publishing Co., 1943.
10. Dom Gregory Dix, *The Shape of the Liturgy*. Dacre, 1945.
11. Charles de Tolnay, *The Sistine Ceiling (Michelangelo)*. Princeton University Press, 1951.
12. Stephen Spender, *World within World*. Harcourt, Brace and Company, Inc., 1951.
13. Benjamin P. Thomas, *Abraham Lincoln*. Alfred A. Knopf, 1952.
14. I Sam. 5:3.
15. Mark 5:23.
16. II Pet. 3:11.

V. The Preacher as Craftsman

1. Rudyard Kipling, *Something of Myself*. Doubleday & Company, 1937.
2. S. I. Hayakawa, *Language in Action*. Harcourt, Brace and Company, Inc., 1941.
3. Ezek. 33:32 (A.V.).
4. *Collected Poems*, 1951. Copyright, 1951, by The Macmillan Company, and used by permission.
5. H. W. Schwartz, *The Story of Musical Instruments*. Doubleday & Company, 1943.
6. Luke 18:2.
7. Luke 3:10.
8. Acts 2:37.
9. Eccles. 12:13 (A.V.).
10. Acts 22:6.
11. Acts 26:12–13.
12. C. E. Montague, *A Writer's Notes on His Trade*. Doubleday & Company, 1930.
13. Richard Niebuhr in *The Christian Century*, July 23, 1930.

VI. Preaching During an Earthquake

1. A. T. Olmstead, *Jesus in the Light of History.* Charles Scribner's Sons, 1942, pp. 254, 258.
2. Douglass S. Freeman in *The Churchman.*
3. Luke 10:1.
4. Audrey Wurdemann, *Splendour in the Grass.* Copyright, 1936, by Harper & Brothers, and used by permission.
5. Mark 13:1.
6. William O. Douglas, *Strange Lands and Friendly People.* Harper & Brothers, 1951.